Jawid Danish is an Afghan v
2015. He is a student, now in
politics, a writer and public sp   activist. This is his
first book, written so he could tell the story of his journey
from his home in Baghlan to his new life in Helsinki. He has
also spent a lot of time in Greece and is a fan of swimming
in the Aegean and playing chess for hours in his favourite
cafés. He is planning on a career that includes a focus on
social justice and human rights.

Kathleen Macdonell has helped Jawid Danish with writing
his first book. She had a career in education in the US before
moving to Greece five years ago. In Athens, she continues
her work in education by helping young refugees have
access to school and university; she is the director of a
scholarship program for refugees at the American College of
Greece and works together with other NGOs to design
programs to improve access to education. She is a human
rights activist working for dignity and justice for the most
vulnerable.

To my family and my long-suffering country.

JAWID DANISH AND
KATHLEEN MACDONELL

LONG WAY FROM HOME

AUSTIN MACAULEY PUBLISHERS™
LONDON • CAMBRIDGE • NEW YORK • SHARJAH

A CIP catalogue record for this title is available from the British Library.

ISBN 9781398465381 (Paperback)
ISBN 9781398465398 (ePub e-book)

www.austinmacauley.com

First Published 2023
Austin Macauley Publishers Ltd®
1 Canada Square
Canary Wharf
London
E14 5AA

To the Finnish people who have welcomed me and made me feel at home in their country.

My thanks to Mr Peter Welch, who believed in me from the first moment we met.

Introduction

My name is Jawid. I came to Europe as a refugee from Afghanistan and I have been living in Finland for the past two years. In many ways, I am the luckiest of those who made the journey; I am a student in an international school in Helsinki, I have found a mother, I have many friends who are Finnish, Afghan, and from all over the world, I live in a comfortable home and have all the food and clothes that I need. I can see my future; three more years of high school and then a good university and a professional career in front of me.

I have seen the other side too; a friend who deported himself back to Afghanistan and many refugees who have been unwillingly deported back to Afghanistan to face violence and even death. Viktoria Square in Athens is filled with lost souls wandering around, lost because they have been in Europe for several years and have not yet taken even the first steps towards integration and now are without hope. There are many students who have not been able to resume their disrupted education and families who are separated by bureaucratic rules at a time when they are all so vulnerable.

And yet even I, the luckiest of the lucky, sometimes have trouble figuring out who I am. How do I combine the six-year-old boy who had to walk cows up to pasture in the mountains outside of my little Afghan village with the 16-year-old who is learning to ice skate on the outdoor rinks of Helsinki? How do I talk to my brothers, still in that village, and describe to them my life, when they have no way to really comprehend many of the things I want to tell them? How can I describe my life at school to my sister when we are talking after a Taliban attack just happened in the street outside her home? How can I explain to people who I am, when as soon as they hear I am a refugee, they have images of people getting off the boats in Lesvos or Chios or Samos and don't understand that, although those boat trips may have been the most terrifying part of the journey for people who didn't know how to swim, those boat trips were just the final steps after months and months of frightening border crossings, long hikes through snow-covered mountains or through deserts of unbearable heat, of cramped trips in cars and pick-up trucks, of imprisonment and of threats and of hunger and thirst?

And so, I am writing this book. I want to remember all the things that happened to me on my journey from Afghanistan to Europe. I was just 12 when I left and now at 16, already I am forgetting some of the things I lived through. Another reason is to describe my life to my classmates, teachers, friends, and even to psychologists I have worked with, since none of them has the background information to really understand what I have gone through. Writing this book has also been a source of therapy for me, allowing me to remember the things I have gone through and face them, accept them, and incorporate them into my psyche. But the biggest reason is to join my voice to the voices of others who have written books, made films, written poems, drawn pictures, and made paintings in an effort to let the world know what this experience has been. I want people to know our stories and accept us as the complicated people we are, complicated just as all human beings are, exceptional perhaps because we have experienced some of the most extreme things that people can experience.

And yet, what we want is what all people want, to live in peace, with dignity and hope. It seems that my life will unfold on the continent of Europe, and I am grateful for that. But I can't forget my family and friends in Afghanistan and I want them to have the same possibility of dignity and hope for a future in an Afghanistan at peace. Because most of all, I miss my home and want to see the suffering of all the people there end.

Chapter 1
At Home in Afghanistan

If no one had a real football, then we played with a ball made from scraps of plastic or fabric, or with an empty Coca Cola bottle that we found lying around. There were two spots in our neighbourhood for these games, one was the dusty, dry, open space outside our village, a space that had provided for years the basic dirt and mud needed for the construction of our homes and was left empty of all grass and plants. The second area was inside the village, in a large garden that had an empty space really too small for a football game, but we had learned to adapt. The dusty space was very tough for us since most of us played barefoot; we would go home with cuts on our feet from the stones embedded in the dirt and with clothes so filthy our mothers would be completely frustrated with us. The field in the garden was easier on us in some ways; the challenge there was playing on a field with an irregular shape, mostly rectangular but with a triangle on one side that rose to an elevation almost a metre higher than the main part of the rectangle. The strongest boy or the guy who brought a real football with him got to make all the decisions about the game. The goalie was always the pudgiest kid on the street. We had no coach, and we played fiercely, too fiercely, from our mothers' point of view. There were no time limits to the match; we played until we were all exhausted or until someone broke a leg or dislocated a toe. When it was just the boys from our village, we didn't care much about the score; we played for our love of the game. But when we had matches with boys from neighbouring villages, then it became brutal. We weren't playing just for ourselves; each of our teams represented their neighbourhood and we fought to uphold our honour with as much determination as any soldier ever fought to defend his country. We always played with a feeling of careless freedom, but at the same time there was the knowledge that anything could happen at any time. Although we were children and didn't yet know about fear, we did know that our world was marked by bombs, attacks, guns, bodies clad in *kafan*, our word for shrouds, waiting for the grave.

That was then, 2013. Baghlan province, in the east of Afghanistan, between Kabul and Mazar Sharif, is best known for the sugar factory that produces the highest quality sugar in Afghanistan. Those football games were so different from the ones in my life now. As a student at the International School of Helsinki, I play on beautifully groomed fields in a blue uniform with matching socks and with new cleats. Just five years have passed since those games in my village, and now I play at schools all over Helsinki and even have had the opportunity to travel with my high-school team to other European countries.

I'm sitting right now in a café in a beautiful square in Athens, working on this book with my mother. We had a good lunch, I drank my cappuccino, and will go home to a full refrigerator. I am visiting Greece to spend a month with my mother. I live in Helsinki, have a Finnish resident permit for the next four years, and I have papers that allow me to travel within the Schengen zone. I speak and do my studies in

English, I can hold a conversation in Finnish, and have grown used to the lifestyle of European countries.

My dream

I am noticing that I have nothing in common with my brothers in Afghanistan; I don't understand this, and when we speak, I have nothing to say. I feel really guilty about this; I never call them and when I do, I just don't know what to say and how to respond to them. They talk about making bricks to fix the house and working in the mud. When they tell me this, they proudly say, "Look, Jawid, we are working." My life is so completely different.

When I touch something, it is clean but they are up to their knees in mud, stamping the mud to make it soft and pliable to build the walls of their house. This is what their lives are about. If I told them about my life, they would not be able to imagine what we are learning. For example, in one of my classes, we are designing and talking about how to decorate the classroom, what colour it should be, what kind of couch we want to have, if there should be plants in the room. By contrast, when I was in Afghanistan, the students would fight over a small piece of carpet so that we did not have to sit on the dirt floor. How can I speak to my brothers about my soft, clean, privileged school where the teachers do not use beating sticks, a place where the students can choose the kind of sofa they would like to have, where the classes consist of just 10 or 15 students rather than 35 or 40 in one room, or about having my own laptop and working online rather than carrying 18 books. I spend a lot of my time in a place where the students can play video games during break, can go and check out a book from the school library, can run to the field for a quick game of football, or can just hang out with all the boys and girls together. I cannot share this with them, and I have nothing to say because they would not be able to imagine. They are struggling to stay alive as Hazara in Afghanistan where people are killed every day.

If I shared my experience of life with them today, we would all feel bad; the comparison and contrast would be so great that the burden of it would be too heavy to carry inside myself. I feel it here, in my belly, and it hurts. But there is a part of me that pulls me to call them, to try to keep them close, to preserve the relationship. And so I answer when they call, and when they complain that I never call them, I just blame the internet and tell them that they are always offline. I lie to them and it hurts a lot. This is how I understand it or justify it, so that I can carry this burden.

Last night, I had a dream in which my two brothers were in Helsinki. Strangely, they came on a plane without their wives. We were walking in the streets of Helsinki with a woman I did not recognise. I was showing my brothers the city. We went to the sauna, and I described to them the sauna tradition in Finland. We walked past libraries and theatres, saw women not wearing burkas in the streets, women walking hand-in-hand with men, no sign of tanks or soldiers, Chinese and Thai and Turkish and Mexican restaurants, swimming pools and skating rinks, beautiful stone buildings, some surrounded by carefully tended gardens, clean streets, buses and trams and trolleys and the metro, all of these things, so familiar to any European but strange and unfamiliar to them. Here they were not knee-deep in mud but rather bathing and relaxing in the sauna, not walking on the dusty, gun-filled streets of Afghanistan but rather walking in safety, without fear or expectation of the next suicide bomb.

In this dream, I shared with them the experiences and moments of my life here that would be impossible for me to put into words if they hadn't seen them with their own eyes.

When did my journey really begin?

I arrived in Finland on 12 June 2017, after ten months in Greece. I was first sent to a shelter for unaccompanied minors in the central part of the country but was allowed to go to Helsinki once I was accepted into the eighth grade at the International School of Helsinki. My first year in this school was intense. I loved every minute of it but I struggled greatly. I knew some English but wasn't really ready for the IB curriculum the school followed. Additionally, I was a boy with a story very different from any of my classmates. I had never been to an international school and had no idea what that meant but I found a very welcoming community with students from all around the world and a faculty that was ready to help me at every step. The faculty and administration knew my background but the students didn't. I wanted them to see me first as their friend, teammate, and classmate before they knew my story. I soon ended up with friends from Finland, Spain, Russia, the U.S., China, India, Sweden, and Ireland.

My English improved rapidly. I was never shy about asking my teachers for extra explanations and I quickly learned enough slang to have good conversations with my friends during lunch and breaks. I spent hours watching YouTube videos and movies to learn conversational English.

All that is so far from the baby born in a tiny village in Baghlan province 16 years ago. My family was big, with eight children. I was the youngest. I never met my father and I have only seen one black-and-white photograph of him; he was wearing a turban and a hat, with a distinguished round face, and with a full beard and moustache. As background in the faded photo is a large building, a monument to an important prophet or imam. That was completely appropriate since he was an imam and he had been teaching many of the children of our village. Many children graduated from his classes and when they grew up, they told me that he had been a great imam, that he was the one who had taught them to read and write, and that he was very famous in his time in our area. While my father was teaching children, he also had another job as a gardener. His salary was enough for him to feed his family and live comfortably.

But then, just a few months before I was born, the first tragedy struck. My father had recently met a guy and they had started becoming friends. One day my father had collected some money to buy rice for the family, when suddenly, his new friend appeared and said he could help him since he knew a shopkeeper who was selling rice at a very good price. My father trusted him and so they went off together. We never saw him again. He never came home. My family looked for him for nine days. On the ninth day, my family received a letter telling where his body could be found. They rushed to the place and found his body, mutilated by knife and gun wounds. We never really knew why he was killed. What we think is that it was because my father was the imam, and had stood up to protect the village when it was under attack by the

Taliban. Maybe they thought they could take the village more easily if they got rid of the imam.

In the first few years following my father's death, my mother had to struggle to find ways to keep her children fed and clothed. With so many children, this was an immense task. I don't know how she, as a woman in a small village, managed to accomplish this and I admire her so much. I do know that she was very resourceful; we would run cows up to pastures in the mountains, and we also helped nearby farmers harvest their crops. Then there were times when we wove rugs in the living room of our house. We lived very simply. And all the children did whatever work they could to help her out.

This was not just the story of my family. After so many decades of war, many women were left alone in the same situation as my mother, forced to raise a family on their own, weighed down not just by grief and the immensity of the task but also by a traditional society that left them few options for making money. And so the children had to play a large role in finding enough money to support their families. In my village, I did not know of any child who did not work polishing shoes, making carpets, running the cows to the mountains, hoeing grass for the cows. It was normal for children to work instead of going to school because we were a population of orphaned children, families of children parenting each other, children working to feed their families.

I don't know exactly where my mother was born, although I do know that she and her family moved to Baghlan when she was a teenager. When she was 17 years old, my father showed up in her village and heard about her. He asked her father if he could marry her. My grandfather learned everything he could about him; what kind of person he was, what kind of family he came from, what kind of job he had. My grandfather was happy with what he learned, and so he let him marry his daughter.

This had all happened according to Afghan custom. In Afghanistan back then, and still today, when a man wants to marry a young woman, he has to go and ask the father for permission. Usually before he does this, he asks friends and neighbours of the girl all about the family so he can understand what kind of a girl she is. At times like this, the whole family, parents, grandparents, aunts, uncles, get involved.

Of course, I was not at my parents' wedding. But from what I have heard from friends and neighbours, the wedding was a typical Afghani one, with three days of celebration. On the second night before the wedding, the entire village joins in the preparations; some people do the cleaning, others cook, others set up the tables and bring out the glasses and plates. On the night before the wedding, there is a big party at the bride's house. The bride and the groom sit on a stage, dressed in special clothing, with their hands hennaed in intricate designs, to exchange their rings. Then the groom is taken to his home by all the young men, and the bride stays at her home surrounded by all the young women. After this, there is dancing to traditional Afghani music in both groups and the dancing continues late into the night.

The actual wedding ceremony takes place when the imam is present. He presides over the ceremony, says the wedding prayers, and the words that officially announce their union. This can actually take place at any stage of the engagement but most families prefer for it to happen on the night that the hands are hennaed. The wedding day itself starts out with dancing by the young men at the groom's house and by the young women at the bride's house. After several hours, the groom then goes to the bride's house where there is a big feast for all the people who have been invited. When the party is over, he returns to his home with his bride. I'm not sure how my father made this trip in those days, probably by horse. Nowadays, the car carrying the newly married couple is decorated by the groomsmen and is the first car in a long procession of other cars of the wedding guests that follow with lots of honking and yelling and competition to be the car closest to the bride and groom.

Although I do not know the exact details of my parents' wedding, I am sure that theirs was similar to this tradition. And I do know that after the wedding, they lived in Akhtar's village, which remained the family home for many years.

In the years that followed, my mother gave birth to eight children. I was the last child. My father was killed when my mother was pregnant with me, and so I know very little about that time.

I was born Hazara, a minority people in Afghanistan. There are three major groups in Afghanistan: Hazara, Pashtuns, and Tajiks. Pashtuns and Tajiks are followers of Sunni Islam, while we, the Hazara, follow the Shia branch. The origins of the Hazara are unclear. Some claim, and most Hazara believe, that they are native to Afghanistan while others theorise that they are descendants of Genghis Khan and the Mongol empire. We speak Dari, a form of Farsi.

There is a long history of antipathy between Pashtuns and Hazara. The area where we lived was mostly all Pashtun and Tajiks. Only our village had a significant population of Hazara, and that's why some people called it Hazaras' village instead of its real name, Akhtar's village.

The guy who killed my father was a Pashtun, and we think that that is one of the reasons he targeted my father.

In recent years, as the Taliban have taken over more and more of the country, they have gotten closer and closer to my village. In the years just before I left, they were attacking my village; people had to run to the fields and mountains to save their lives. The Taliban were fierce and had no compunction about killing any person they found in their path. Our lives became more and more difficult and I was scared even to go to school.

Actually, I use the word 'Taliban' but the real situation is that no one has ever been completely clear about the people who claim to be 'Taliban'. The organisation originally was a Sunni Islamic fundamentalist group that arose in the '90s, whose members had been students educated in Pashtun areas in conservative Islamic schools, after fighting in the Soviet-Afghan war. The Taliban had received weapons and military training from the US to help them in their cause of driving the Russians out. But after that war, its adherents grew more diverse and it became more of an informal insurgency that attracted all kinds of fundamentalists who wanted to impose their strict laws on the entire population of Afghanistan. Violence in Afghanistan has been endemic for decades, and some criminals commit murder and other violence in the name of the Taliban, without having any connection to the group, just to gain some sense of purpose for their random acts of violence.

Before things became so difficult, I had a normal Afghani childhood. I had friends all over the village, I loved football and riding my bike and playing marbles and flying kites. I was a very serious student. My friends always laughed at me because I always had a book with me wherever I went. And I was named the top student in my class every year. I was following my brothers in that way; they also were very smart and serious about their studies.

When I was 5 years old, the second tragedy hit my family. Two of my brothers were killed by a Taliban suicide bomber. All the students from the school had been gathered in the street in front of the Sugar Factory to celebrate the presence of an important politician who had plans to re-open the building after a long renovation. Present also at the celebration were some members of the National Assembly. School children had lined up on both sides of the street that led to the Sugar Factory to greet the delegation; at that moment a suicide bomber approached the group and then set off his bomb. The politician and his six guards were killed, and a large number of students as well. In all, nearly 75 people were killed in that attack, 59 of them children, and among them were two of my brothers.

I narrowly missed being a victim myself. I was there with the school children even though I hadn't yet started school. My brother Zaher saw me there and told me to go home. I started crying that I wanted to stay but my brother asked some neighbours to take me home. We had just reached the door of our house, and my hand was on the handle when we heard the explosion.

My sister and my brother's wife rushed to the door to see what had caused all the noise.

Darkness and swirling dust and confusion were all around us even though my house was nearly a kilometre from the Sugar Factory. Neighbours ran out of their houses in panic, trying to understand what was going on. The explosion was followed by gunfire that we could clearly hear from our house. In the confusion, the bodyguards of the politicians and the police who were present started shooting, hoping that they would be killing the people responsible for the bombing but not really able to distinguish the perpetrators from the bystanders. We learned later that this was how my brothers died; my older brother had been shot by three bullets on his abdomen and back, and my other brother had just a single shot to his head.

My nearest neighbour, Latif, a tall gentle guy in his late 30s, ran up to our house. His usual smile was gone and instead his face reflected fear and concern. From his experience, he knew what was coming next as every family pulled out their donkey-driven carts to go to the scene and help collect the bodies. He spoke firmly to me and told me to get permission from my sisters to get our cart so we could go to the Sugar Factory to help. I'm not sure if he exactly knew that something had happened to my brothers but he was insistent that I go with him. At the moment I was the only male in the house.

Halfway to the street that led to the Sugar Factory, we were met with the sight of carts and cars already filled with the bodies of our friends and families. The driver of one of the cars saw me sitting on the seat of our cart and told Latif to take me home. I didn't know then what was going on but I realised it when we finally arrived back home and saw my brothers' bodies, hard to recognise because they were covered in blood, being taken out of the car. Some of the men in the car were carefully placing my brothers on blankets so they could carry them into the house. I was standing there taking all this in. I don't remember feeling anything, probably because I was so young with no idea of what death meant. I do remember all our neighbours coming up to me and hugging me and I was a little bewildered by that.

Even though I was only 5, I have very clear pictures in my mind of all of this. The one thing that haunts me is that last conversation with my brother. We had quarrelled because I had been so stubborn and hadn't wanted to leave. And that was the last conversation I ever had with him. I have regretted that ever since that time. I wish that that last conversation had been one of love and laughter instead.

My mother learned of their deaths when she returned home from the fields where she had been picking cotton. She understood that something was wrong when she saw crowds of people at the entrance to our house. By this time, my brothers had been carried into the house. My mother entered and was immediately overwhelmed with grief; I can still hear her sobbing and wailing. Our home soon filled with relatives from near and far. The bodies of my brothers were laid out in the courtyard of our home. I can remember my mother going from one to the other, uncovering their faces for one more look, one more caress, covering their faces with kisses. The women who came to our home took places next to her and kept trying to restrain her and calm her down. The bodies remained in the courtyard the whole night and my mother did not leave their side. She was in shock, almost lifeless one moment and wringing her hands in agony the next.

My brother Ibrahim finally arrived. He had been up in the mountains preparing the ground for the planting of pistachio trees. He hadn't heard the explosion or heard the news until he reached the village. He had spent the last few hours at work in complete ignorance of the disaster that had hit our family.

When he reached home, he fainted several times until he was able to take over as the oldest man in the family there that day. He struggled with the men who were carrying the bodies of his brothers; he wanted that responsibility to be given to him alone.

The next day my mother was completely drained, she couldn't talk and moved with difficulty. My brothers were buried in the village cemetery. Ibrahim was overcome with the pain of his loss, he didn't want to take the bodies to the cemetery, and after they finally were taken there, he tried to lie down on top of his brothers in the graves; he didn't want to leave his brothers or live without them. After the funeral, my mother made one big decision not to let my eldest brother Jawad know about these deaths. He was 19 at the time and was working in Iran. The income he sent home was critical for the support of our family. It was nearly a year later when he finally found out, through a random program on TV. He immediately left Iran and returned home to become the head of the family. In his place, my brother Ibrahim left for Iran to find a job in order to send money back to us.

I don't really remember the details of the next few years. My mother continued to work; she found it a relief to be with other women. She was consumed by her memories; every street, every corner, every part of the house reminded her of her lost children, and had the ability to move her to collapse in sobs. I do remember that she kept getting smaller and smaller.

She seemed to be disappearing in front of our eyes.

After a while we realised that the weight loss was due to something more than grief. There were no doctors in our area who had the ability to make a diagnosis, so my brothers took her to Mazar Sharif and to Kabul to see specialists there. One of the last doctors to see her revealed to my aunt's husband that it was cancer and that it was incurable. It was impossible for my brothers to believe this and they wanted to take her to Pakistan for better medical care. But my aunt's husband finally persuaded them that the trip would be too difficult for her and that there was no hope for a cure. So, my brothers brought her home. Jawad continued to lead the family and help us cope, and Ibrahim, who had returned home when he learned how sick my mother was, gave my mother the tenderest care possible. She couldn't move and Ibrahim was the one who picked her up and carried her outside when she had to go to the bathroom. He made all kinds of fruit juices to entice her to drink something. But she soon reached a point when she could no longer eat, so her treatment was nutrition through an IV. The only other medication was to alleviate the pain.

She remained in this condition for about six months.

My mom had lost the ability to talk or walk. What I remember was that she had become so thin that we could see her bones. It became clearer and clearer that she did not have long to live. She died one evening at 11 pm. I was sleeping at the time. I was awakened by crying throughout the house. I was eight years old.

For the next few years, Jawad became my father and my mother, with responsibility for the whole family. Jawad, as the eldest child, 21 years old, took over the care of the five of us; my sister, Zaher's daughter, my brothers Ibrahim and Alijan, and me. My grandmother was there for us too, although she was not with us all the time. She alternated weeks; one week with us, and the next with my aunt, helping her with the care of my five cousins. When I think of my grandmother, I remember that she was very tall and thin and blind in one eye because when she was a girl, she had to break branches for firewood and one time a branch accidentally damaged her eye. She could not read or write because she had not gone to school, so when there was a book or paper in the house, she would put this to good use in making fires. I remember her as a practical woman who used her resources to keep us warm and fed. Her mobility was hampered by asthma and she often needed to sit down and use her inhaler. We took care of each other; I would be the one to bring her drops for her eye or her asthma pump, and she would also save food leftover from the previous night for me. I always felt very close to her and was filled with grief and regret when I learned of her death several months ago. Grief because I missed sharing my life with her these past few years, and regret for the times I had been stubborn and given her a hard time. When I left Afghanistan, she said that her greatest wish was to see us married and happy with our own children. It makes me so sad that she won't be here to see this for me.

Together, my grandmother and Jawad took care of the family. Jawad was doing his best, stepping into the place of my parents to prevent me from hanging out with kids who might be a bad influence. Whenever I wanted to go and play football, he would say, "No, do your school work or come and help me at the kiosk." He made sure that he kept me safe and close but sometimes I found a way to sneak out by the back of our house, over the fallen wall of the neighbour's house, and when he was looking the other way, I would run as fast as I could through the forest to the playground. It was a roundabout way but I usually made it to the field to enjoy a game of football.

Jawad was so good to me. He made sure that I attended school every day and promised me that no matter what, he would make sure that I continued at school. I worked with him in the kiosk in front of our house; I loved him and looked up to him. He provided me with a safe space and with guidance while my family reeled from the loss of my mother.

The next five years for me were very tough. I wanted to focus on school but it was difficult; my family was quarrelling with each other, I had to work, and the violence in the country threatened us at every moment. My days were full; I had to run the cows up to the pastures in the mountains, I had to come home and help make carpets, and after that, I had to help Jawad work in the kiosk while trying to keep up with my studies. Despite these challenges, I managed to be named the top student in my class each year, in a class of 36 students. My teachers often asked me to help teach other students. I loved my studies and was very ambitious, and I wanted to study as much as I could and for as long as I could.

My school in Afghanistan could not be more different from my school in Finland. There were many good teachers, to be sure. But there were also *ostad seven-kilo kachalo* (Teacher seven-kilo Potatoes), *ostad biscuit lola* (Teacher Rolled Cookies,) and *ostad gandana* (Teacher Chives). Those teachers had earned their names according to the kind of bribes they had been known to accept as a price for a high grade. Another shortcut to a good grade was good calligraphy that ensured that the teachers would be so influenced by the beauty of your writing that they would not pay too much attention to the content.

As I got older, I was expected to contribute in a new way to our family's finances. During the last few months of my time in Afghanistan, I began to work in the Sugar Factory near the spot where my two brothers had been killed. I hadn't earned any money from the work that I had done before; making carpets and running the cows and working in the kiosk were just things that I did to keep our family enterprises up and running. So, my brother wanted me to work in the factory in order to learn not only how to earn real money but also to see what it was like to actually earn money for a living. For the first time during those months, I made money and gave it to my brother to help take care of the family or to buy clothes or food.

Up until the time I started there, I had never thought that I would find myself working at the Sugar Factory. It had always been a big employer in our area; many families owed their livelihood to the salaries they earned from their jobs there. The director of the factory was one of our close neighbours, so my brother Jawad arranged for them to hire me. At first, my job was hard physical labour, working the night shift from 6 pm until 6 am. There was sugar leftover from the previous year's production, and over the course of the year, it had turned into hard masses. My job was to break up these huge blocks of hardened, old sugar and pulverise them into small grains that would eventually be combined with the current year's production. Despite the fact that many of us working this backbreaking job were just kids, there was a supervisor who walked among us the entire night, threatening any one of us who was slacking off with a loss of pay or with the loss of the job. This was the hardest work I had ever done so far, not knowing that I would face harder when I finally reached Iran.

Luckily, after working there for just three or four nights, one of the directors of the Sugar Factory came to me. "Are you the son of Shaikh Qorban? You are the one who is doing so well in school?" I confirmed that I was. "We need someone who is good at math to work in the laboratory." So, I escaped the hard labour and took up a new job in the lab, using the equipment to test the quality of the sugar that was going through the production process each night. This was really fun for me and made me feel important since we were responsible for making sure that the production equipment was working properly, based on our analysis of the sugar coming out of it. We had to do numerous tests on each batch of sugar hourly but the tests didn't take that long, so we ended up having lots of downtime as we waited for the next batch. Usually, there were just two of us, the engineer and me. He taught me a lot during this time. This was actually the first time I learned about the internet and the first time I ever saw a site called Facebook. I felt proud that I had heard about Skype, although I had to ask him what it was.

My life in other ways was the same as children around the world. I loved football, loved hanging out with my friends, and loved riding my bike all over the village. I was reminded of this recently when I agreed to work at the summer day camp for younger students sponsored by my school in Helsinki. I was the only student helper, and I worked with the director to keep a group of kids, ranging from four to seven years old, involved in the activities and engaged with the program each day. I was struck by how much they were like me at that age, a surprise to me, since I had grown up in such a different culture. They fought to be first in line, they cried when someone else got in their way, they were happiest running around and bumping into each other and climbing trees, they cried if someone stepped on their shadow. But I also kept thinking about how different they were from me; they all had homes with parents, they didn't have to work, they had many clothes and lots of food, and had opportunities like summer camp, which was something I had never even heard of before. The days I spent with them became very emotional for me as I remembered the young child I had been and for the first time, perhaps, realised what a difficult life I had had when I was their age.

My difficulties as a young child in Afghanistan grew more and more intense until I reached the age of 12 and realised that I had to leave my country. Obviously, this was a very difficult decision and Jawad and I had a long conversation on the day he told me I had to leave so that I would be safe.

There were four main reasons it was necessary for me to leave.

For the previous two years, the situation with the Taliban was getting worse day by day. The Taliban had been in opposition to the government for years. They arose from the chaos after the Russians were forced to leave the country and their goals were to impose a radical Islamic rule over all of Afghanistan and to expel all foreign forces. Intense fighting between the government and the Taliban had been going on for many years but the fighting was coming closer and closer to our part of the country. Gradually, some cities near us, Kunduz and Baghlan, were falling to the Taliban and experiencing their violence not only against government soldiers but also civilians, women, and children. People in my village had to stay vigilant at all times and took lots of steps to stay safe, shops would close quickly when news spread of Taliban in the area, people avoided large groups for fear of suicide bombers, and there was a curfew each night, but the violence was unpredictable and people were killed every day. The government could not be relied on to protect the population, even though there was a military base right next to the Sugar Factory. It was a period of intense terror for all of us.

In addition to this kind of fear, the small Hazara community in Baghlan was always afraid of the Pashtuns, who were in the majority. In my school, I was one of only ten Hazara, among over 2000 students in my school. The Pashtun students were always making fun of me and bullying me; in my class, students called me "Hazara" and not "Jawid". Sometimes they called me "Chinese" or "Japanese" or "Flat-nosed" and made fun of my almond-shaped eyes. They taunted me and told me to go back to those countries; one characteristic of Hazara people is that we have some similarities in appearance with people from the far east. They also would surround me in the classroom and make fun of me because I was Shia and they were Sunni: why did we pray in such funny ways? Why do we believe that Ali was the correct successor to Mohammed? Why do we celebrate the anniversary of the cruel murders of Imam Hassan and Imam Hussain? Once on my way to school, a Pashtun guy who was holding a knife came up to me and told me that he was going to kill me. I managed to escape by screaming for help. I was proud of my Hazara heritage, and I even loved it when they called me "Hazara" because everyone knew me and knew that I was such a good student. It made me happy that I was a good representative of my people. I don't mean by this to make it sound like we were against the Pashtuns; we all had many connections with them since we lived in such a small community. Even today, among the immigrant communities in Europe, we all see ourselves as Afghans first, rather than Hazara or Pashtun, and we connect at that level.

My father's killer was also a threat to me and to my other brothers. As we got older, he was afraid of us, afraid we would take revenge on him. We feared that he was eager to kill us so that he could end his fear of us.

Perhaps the biggest reason, though, has to do with my extended family and their threat against me. There was a serious issue between some members of my family and some distant cousins. The result of this was that those distant cousins started threatening my brother's life. He fled to Europe. But then those cousins turned against me and started threatening to kill me. One day when I was in school, my teacher came to tell me to leave quickly and go home, that there were some people coming to the front of the school, crashing through the guards, and that they were looking for me. I no longer felt safe in school or anywhere in my village.

For one week, Jawad would not let me out of his sight, not even to go to school. Finally, he told me those heavy words that I had to leave in order to be safe. He gave me the equivalent of $50 and told me that he could no longer protect me and so I had to leave to protect myself.

On my last night at home, I went to see my good friend Gholam Nabi. We did everything together and never had any secrets from each other. He would come to my house and help me while I was making carpets and the next day I would go to his house and help him. We often slept over at each other's house. He was like a brother to me. He told me that I just needed to get to Kabul and that he had a family friend there who would smuggle me to Iran. Europe was not in my mind at all. I just wanted to get to Iran where there were many Afghans living and where I could be safe. I had no idea of the difficulties of Afghans living in Iran, no idea of how far the journey would be, or what it would be like. My only thoughts were about how to be safe and about how sad I felt leaving my family and my home.

I really had no preparations to make; I had a small backpack from school. I put one t-shirt in it, and one pair of jeans, since I knew that Iranians did not wear Afghani style clothing and I wanted to blend in. I had only the shoes I was wearing, a pair of sneakers. No food, because I was sure that I could find food while I was still in Afghanistan.

Gholam Nabi invited several of our friends to his home that night. We played cards and talked about all of our memories, all the good times we had had, our long walks to school kicking stones and playing games with pencils, all the football we had played together, all the kites we had flown and caught, and all the marble competitions we had had. Gholam Nabi was very emotional, saying that he felt lonely since so many of his friends had left and now I was going too. Although it was never safe to be out in the streets of our village late at night, that night they all walked me home at about 1 am. These boys were the only people who knew I was leaving; it was a secret I couldn't entrust to anyone else. I couldn't even say goodbye to my teachers, or to my friends in school. I wondered about what my teachers thought since I hadn't been in school for a week. Normally I was a very responsible student, the one who always brought the chalk

34

and erasers and the attendance book into the classroom. Were they wondering where I was?

When I arrived home, Jawad was the only one who was awake. We sat and talked not like brothers would do, but he spoke to me like a father, since that was the role he had played in my life for so many years. I can't even imagine how hard that all was for him, having to send his 'son' away from the family but knowing that that was the only way to keep him safe.

And so at the age of 12, I left my family, my friends, my home, my village, my country.

Chapter 2
My Journey Begins – In Afghanistan

I woke up early in the morning, about 4 am. My sister heard that I was up, ran to me, and started crying; it killed me because she was the one I was closest to in the family. In the midst of her tears, she told me that she hadn't slept at all because she had been thinking of me all night. I hugged her and cried too. I was pulled in two opposite ways. On the one hand, I was very emotional about leaving my family and my home but on the other hand, I had already steeled myself against the pain that I knew was coming with my departure. As I look back now, I am struck by how simple it felt then. At that time, I had no idea of the long journey I had in front of me, or of the dangers and difficulties I would face.

I didn't eat any breakfast but finally said my goodbyes and then walked secretly in the dark to the main street of the area and positioned myself on the side of the road where the cars looking for riders who wanted to go to Pol Khomri were driving by. I waved down a car, got in, and was on my way.

When we reached Pol Khomri, I still felt comfortable. This is a city I had visited many times before with my brothers when they went there to go shopping for products for our kiosk. I was dropped off at a square lined with cars headed in different directions. 'Kabul', 'Mazar' and 'Kunduz' were the city names shouted out by the drivers who were looking for passengers to their destination. I was walking alongside all the waiting cars, when a taxi driver who has headed to Kabul saw me and shouted, *"Bachim, koja meri."* ("My son, where do you want to go?")

He was a scary guy to me, maybe 50 years old or so, with a big paunch and with a long beard and a turban wrapped around his head. I responded to his question: *"Kabul merum, kaka jan."* ("I'm going to Kabul, dear uncle.") I was nervous and anxious, and my voice cracked. This was my first experience in a situation like this. His car was a Toyota Corolla; I climbed into the back seat behind the driver and was soon joined by three other people. Two of them took seats with me in the back and the other one sat upfront with the driver. The conversation between them and the driver was all about checkpoints and raids by armed bandits and the memorials lining the roads to mark the spots where people had been martyred by the Taliban or killed during Russian attacks. I listened intently to everything they were saying, and the more I heard, the more frightened I became.

We finally reached Kabul at about one in the afternoon.

I had been there once before, when the highlight of my visit had been walking through the streets of the big city of Kabul at night with my cousin. This time, I arrived all alone, and the car dropped me off in Kote Sangi, a big intersection on the southwest side of the city. I immediately headed over to a nearby restaurant where I knew a friend of our family was working. I met him there and he fed me and then directed me to the place where I would meet the guy who would smuggle me to Iran. I took a bus from Kote Sangi to Dashte-barchi, a

Hazara neighbourhood in Kabul where the smuggler lived. When I got off the bus, he was there waiting for me. He took me to his house. I stayed there for that night and the next day until five in the afternoon. At that point, the smuggler gave me an address and told me to take a bus from Dashte-barchi to the place where buses to the border leave. By now, I was feeling completely overwhelmed and scared, a 12-year-old on my own, entrusting my fate to strangers, about to travel across borders I had never seen before. I missed my home and kept wondering about how Jawad was feeling.

I found the correct bus, rode it across the city, and finally arrived at the big bus station at nine in the evening. The bus station was chaotic, filled with kids, families, young men with backpacks, all on journeys similar to mine. Young women sat in corners, feeding little pieces of bread to their children, kids were running around chasing each other, young men were walking around aimlessly, some people made little tents from their shawls and rested under those. The whole place was filthy, the smell was awful, and there were flies all around. My bus didn't leave until two in the morning so I was left to wait on my own in the crowded, noisy bus station. I stayed in a waiting room that was nothing more than a ruined structure that looked like it could fall down any second; it was jam-packed with all the people waiting.

Finally, at 2 am, I got on the bus to Nimruz, a province near the Pakistan border. I had to sit far in the back, and I was lucky that I had a seat. That ride taught me a lot; I sat in the back observing everything around me. I overheard conversations all around me; it seemed that no one knew exactly where we were headed. Everyone had a story to tell about why they were leaving, so many stories and yet they were all the same. Fear was in the air. We all knew that we were travelling along routes that were vulnerable to attacks by the Taliban, so the bus travelled fast and made no stops. It was a miracle that the bus survived the trip, since it seemed that it would fall apart at any moment. Luckily, we arrived the next afternoon, having survived the ancient bus and the dangerous roads. We were all famished by the time we arrived and desperately needed to go to the bathroom.

In Nimruz I was met by a province and a climate completely unfamiliar to me and I found myself uncomfortably surrounded only by Pashtuns. The first thing I did when I got off the bus was to try to use the phone that the first smuggler I met in Kabul had given me. I had never even seen a phone like that and I had no idea how to use it. My first call was not to my family but to the next smuggler, the guy who would take me across the border to Iran. He gave me an address but I had no idea how to get to his place. No one around me spoke Dari but luckily, I had learned Pashtu in my village, so I was able to keep asking for directions. Finally, I arrived at his run-down hostel and met the smuggler. The hostel was a huge building, with two or three floors, and with an inner courtyard, also huge, almost the size of an outdoor cinema. There were obviously many people staying there; laundry hung from the windows and people were staring out, watching what was happening below them. When I entered one of the rooms, I saw three other boys, just like me, sitting there, all waiting for the next step of the journey. They didn't know each other either and we all sat there wondering what was going on, nervous, anxious, lost. One of them was very big and the two others were small like me but we were very young, 12 to 15 years old. That night the smuggler cooked an omelette for all of us. There was no conversation because we were all exhausted and a little scared, so we fell asleep on the floor as soon as we finished eating.

The smuggler woke us up at 6 am and gave us another omelette for breakfast, my last meal in Afghanistan. Will I ever have another meal in my country? The smuggler then showed us where to take a shower. I had to shower then because I didn't know when I would have the next opportunity for that but that shower was in a disgustingly dirty, dilapidated ruin some distance from his hostel, and the water was salty and filthy. After that, he showed me where I could buy some *naan* and water for the trip. So, I set off on my journey wearing Afghani dress and sneakers, with one pair of jeans, one t-shirt, some bread and two bottles of water in my backpack. My only other possession was my phone. I used it to send a message to my brother Jawad to tell him that I was starting on the last part of my journey to Iran and to let him know that I wouldn't be able to be in touch again until I was safely in Tehran. His message back to me was to give me a very important number, the phone number of a guy named Omid who might be very helpful to me. He was an Afghan living in Iran who had been deported back to Afghanistan in the previous year. During that time, he had lived with my family for several months before he managed to get back to Iran.

This number turned out to be very precious to me.

After buying the bread and water, I went back to the hostel for a few minutes. Then the smuggler took me and the other boys outside to where a taxi was waiting. As we left his house, he stood at the door with a Koran raised high in his hands while we walked under the Koran, with his prayers for our protection for the next part of our trip. We climbed into the taxi and started off for the border. These were my last moments in my country.

And so my first two experiences with smugglers inside Afghanistan were good ones; these men were kind and did what they could to help us. I would soon learn about other smugglers who did not have those qualities. Luckily, I had as company the three other boys I met that night, and since we had been helped by the same smuggler, we would be in the same group as we were put into the pick-up trucks at the border.

Chapter 3
On the Way to Tehran

Climbing into the taxi was no easy thing. We were shocked when we saw that there were already 12 other people inside, nine piled on top of each other on the back seat, two in the passenger seat, and one awkwardly wedged between the passenger seat and the driver seat, straddling the gearbox. The four of us were forced into the trunk of the taxi with our backpacks. We fit into the space by crouching in a position that resembled the yoga child's pose. We cradled our backpacks to our bellies and drew arms up to our foreheads. We felt like we were being confined in a cave without air or escape. It was a terrifying experience for all of us, and we each claimed that our position was worse than the position of the other three. There was no way to move or lessen the extreme discomfort. As I crouched in the trunk of that taxi, I wondered how much worse it could get. At the time, I didn't know what a child's pose was, but I did learn to accept what couldn't be changed and to surrender to feelings of being trapped and confined. Writing this memory now with all my experience of life in Western Europe, I wonder how strange the idea of 16 passengers and one driver in one car would look in Europe. The journey to the border lasted two hours. There would be worse journeys to come. This was just the beginning.

As we neared the border between Afghanistan and Pakistan (the only route that smugglers used to get to Iran at that time), I had my second shock. We stopped at a big open space, filled with pickup trucks, with mud walls all around, and surrounded by wilderness. It was bizarre, because it looked almost like a regular taxi station but instead of taxis waiting for clients, there were trucks waiting for the people the smugglers were bringing. There were hundreds of Afghans, standing like human cattle, milling around with blank expressions on their faces. Dust filled the air and made it hard to breathe. With every step you took on the dirt, clouds of dust would rise up and clog your eyes and nose and mouth. The place also had the feeling of a market, with vendors selling sunglasses and scarves. It was an odd sight; people wrapped the scarves tightly around their faces with just the tips of their noses visible. It looked like a scene from a zombie movie. Even today, when I hear people talking about horror or zombie movies, I have the feeling that I have actually lived through one.

A smuggler put together a group of 36 of us and loaded us onto a small pickup truck. He was holding a thick, rectangular stick about a metre long. He used this to push people into groups and onto the trucks. If anyone dared to speak or look at him in a questioning way, he would hit them with the stick. I realised that I had entered a new world. Gone were the smugglers who took care of us, replaced by this violent, threatening guy. I felt like crying but knew that I couldn't. I kept thinking about my family and my home and all I wanted was to go back to them. That was impossible though and that left me completely scared, knowing that my fate was in the hands of this thug.

This was the first part of the next 13 days of my journey to Tehran, a journey that included other truck rides, some rides in taxis, and several times that we had to run through the desert on foot. There was no food, and we had barely any water, and so we ate dates from palm trees, and any food we still had left. And throughout the journey, we were fired upon by the Taliban when we were in Pakistan and by Iranian soldiers when we reached Iran. At one point two men from our group were kidnapped by Iranian gunmen and we never saw them again. We had to sleep on the ground with no blankets and the nights were very cold, and the days were very hot but we had no protection from the sun.

A word about the pickup trucks; more than 30 people would be forced onto each truck. The front seats were empty but no one was allowed to sit there unless they paid a large sum of money. Even if one person could be found with enough money, the smuggler wouldn't allow him to sit there unless he could find three more people to pay and sit up there with him. In the back of the pickup, there was no space to sit, barely any space to fit in. Workers for the smugglers with pipes in their hands would surround the truck, give the order to sit down, and hit with a pipe anyone who could not manage to do that. At other times, we all had to get off the pickup truck and push it up a rough mountain road, and as it got moving again, we all had to run to catch up to it and hop on. Those who couldn't run fast enough or who weren't agile enough, were left behind to face their fate in the barren mountains. There are no statistics on how many people lost their lives in this way.

The pickup trucks travelled together in convoys of five or six, raising up asphyxiating clouds of dust. That dust obscured our vision of the other trucks, of the landscape around us, even of the sun. We choked on it and struggled to get enough air. People around me were moaning and crying. It was impossible to move or change position while the truck was careening up and down rough mountain roads. But at the same time, we were bounced around by the abrupt movements of the trucks, and we would lose our balance. Our biggest fear became the fear of falling from the trucks. We knew that meant certain death.

The taxis were not any better. The pickup trucks were used in the mountains and deserts, but when we went through towns or checkpoints, we had to take taxis. 16 of us in a taxi, hours on the road. How do you fit 16 into a taxi? People on the floor, under the driver's feet, in the trunk. Because I was small, I was often the one to be on the floor next to the accelerator pedal or curled up in the trunk with two or three other people. We each had our backpacks also, so in the trunk we would place the backpack on the floor of the trunk and crouch over it with our knees pulled up, our heads touching the bottom, and our backs rounded, struggling for air, like this for hours and hours, over the bumps of badly maintained roads. As we neared a checkpoint, the trunk would quickly open and the driver yell "Run!" We could barely move since we were cramped but we were threatened with beatings if we didn't. We had to get out and run quickly five or six kilometres around the checkpoint so that the taxi could pass through safely. The only good thing about this process was that when we re-joined the taxi, those of us who were fast runners could change our positions for the next part of the trip. At that point, the drivers would just push us into the car so we could take off as quickly as possible. "Afghani *koskash,* get in." *Koskash* was only one of the insulting terms they were using for us. Everyone would rush to the taxi, climb in, and hurry to find the most comfortable position they could, squirming with all the other bodies around them doing the same thing, and of course, with the knowledge that what seemed comfortable then, would become torture after two or three hours in the same position. One time I was among the first to get into a taxi and I found a position sitting on another person. It seemed that this would be a position that was at least bearable but the taxi driver was there, and when he saw me, he slapped me hard on my face with his hand, knocking me out for a moment, leaving me with my right ear ringing and my head spinning.

"Afghani *koskhol, takon nakhor.*" ("Stupid Afghan, sit still and don't move.")

What happened when we needed to go to the bathroom? I really don't know what happened to other people. I never had to go, probably because I had eaten and drunk so little, and also because of the intense fear I was always feeling. There was one guy, though, who somehow managed to find an empty Coca Cola bottle. He peed into it. When the driver found out, he stopped the car, opened the back door, and faced the poor guy.

"Get out, Afghan," he shouted.

"Sir, what happened?" replied the guy, with his head down, unable to look at the driver in his fear.

The driver then said, "*Peder sag, dakhel oun botry chi hast.*" ("Son of a dog, what is inside the bottle?")

The guy was silent, unable to utter even a syllable, while we all watched in terror. Hassan, one of the boys who had come with me, turned and whispered to me, "I have been in

46

Iran before and I know these fucking Iranians don't know what it means to be a human being. They are all asses." I wished I could say something but I was filled with fear. The terror and disgust increased as we all watched the driver force the poor guy to drink his own pee.

The trip through the mountains and deserts of Pakistan and Iran never got easier. We passed days through these landscapes and never saw a single person. But to our surprise after every two or three days, there were random places where tents were set up and people connected to the smugglers were selling food and water. Of course, we had to buy from them; it was the only way to feed ourselves. It also was the clearest picture of the way these smugglers were actually just like businessmen, transporting people across lands and borders gave them numerous ways to profit from them. The most egregious example of this was the fact that we encountered armed men at various spots; they were standing on the side of the road, holding powerful guns. Our pickup truck would stop and we were each forced to pay a small fee to the armed men before we could continue the journey. They also would confiscate any jewellery or other valuables they saw.

There is a high mountain between the border of Pakistan and Iran. Its name, *Kohe Moshkel,* means 'Difficult Mountain'. It is the highest mountain I encountered on the entire journey. The pickup trucks went as far as they could up the foothills of the mountain. After that, we had to walk all the way to the highest point. This took hours. We started early in the morning and reached the pass at the top at seven in the evening.

As we were walking, well-worn shoes broke and fell from the feet of many of the people I was travelling with. Walking barefoot, they tried to navigate the hard, sharp stones with bleeding soles. When we were approaching the peak, the first impression was of an isolated, vast place at the top of the world, with no trees or vegetation but endless views of all the surrounding mountains. To my surprise, though, as I reached the upper edge of the summit, the scene unfolded to reveal around five hundred refugees. Some of them were resting on the ground, others were talking, and others were moving around an informal market buying bread and water. There were also groups scattered around, smoking weed and eating opium to dull their pain. It was here that we had to transfer to a new smuggler for the next stage of the journey. Of course, at each one of these transfers, we had to give more money.

I had become friends with Hassan. He was a little older than I was but he was huge, very tall, with a muscular body, large almond-shaped eyes, and a shaved head. We were opposites since I was small with very thick dark hair. It was good to be with him, since people were afraid of him because of his size.

But that didn't help him in this god-forsaken place. The smuggler came up to him to ask him for money. He had hidden his remaining 500 Afghanis in a secret place in the rope he used for a belt. He told the smuggler that he didn't have any money. The smuggler didn't believe him and kept asking him, more forcefully each time. Hassan kept insisting even when the smuggler slapped him and started ripping his clothes. I knew what Hassan was thinking he knew that we had a rough journey ahead and that he needed his money to buy food and water, and without that he would die. So, he persisted in his refusal, even when the smuggler put his fingers up his rectum to check for anything hidden there. I was standing there watching, feeling dread and terror. I would give anything to have avoided seeing that scene that will stay with me my entire life. When it was my turn, without hesitation, I handed over some of my money to the smuggler.

In order to continue the journey, we had to wait on the mountain until the smugglers were informed by their people about which routes were the safe ones to use that night. Once the smugglers got the word, we had to walk down the mountain in our group until we reached the pickup truck. Each of the smugglers had his own group of people; each group had been assigned names like 'Pomegranate' or 'Potato'. The smuggler would call out the name of the group and we had to somehow find him and get to him with all the people in other groups swirling around looking for their smugglers. There were at least ten groups up at the top of the mountain, so it was easy to get lost and lose contact with your group, a terrifying prospect. This process would be repeated at each point in the journey when we reached the points where we were to be handed over to the next smuggler.

It had been hard for us young boys to get to the top of this mountain but it had been much harder for the younger children, for pregnant women, and for all those who were ill, dehydrated, or undernourished from the journey already. It was even harder going down.

We had to leave at night and so we couldn't see anything, the slope was steep and slippery with rocks falling all around us. I could hear children crying and women trying hard to comfort and reassure them. The sound of these women reminded me of my mother when she would try to get me to sit still and stop crying when she needed to wash my hands after I had been playing in the mud, fierce and comforting at the same time. Or of my sister, as she tended to a big cut on my hand that happened when I was helping her in the kitchen.

As we were making our way down the mountain, Hassan and I were at the back of our group. Even in the dark, I was able to see a guy sitting right in front of us on the ground, leaning his back against a rock. I was worried he would miss the caravan and be stuck in the mountain alone, so I went up to him and said to him that he should get up and come with us now. No reply. I thought maybe he was asleep so I tapped him on his shoulder. To my shock, his body slumped over to the side and I realised that it was cold. "*Jawid, berim. Oun morda,*" said Hassan. ("Jawid, come on, let's go. He's dead.") Then he added, "You'll see this a lot more on this journey. There isn't anything you can do. Just remember to take their food and water before you leave."

We finally reached the bottom of the mountain but things did not get better. There were three pickup trucks waiting for us, so we were put back into groups of 36 or so and forced onto the trucks. The trucks took off quickly and then drove at breakneck speed for the next 12 hours as we crossed into Iran. They careened around each curve, with the tires screeching and losing contact with the road. All of us suffered tremendously from the discomfort and were afraid that at any minute we would be thrown from the truck since it did not have side barriers to keep us securely on the vehicle. Hassan finally came up with a plan. He took several scarves from the people around him and at first tightened them to the bars behind the driver's section. Then he climbed over people and moved to the back of the truck, took up a position on the back step of the truck, and held the sections of the scarves taut. People along the sides held onto the scarves, creating a sort of cloth wall to keep us from falling off the truck. To my amazement, Hassan stayed like that, holding on for dear life but completely dedicated to what he was doing, for hours and hours. He won my greatest respect. I don't know how he fought the fear that he would fall off at any second and be left behind in the dust.

One of the most surprising things to me was the different reactions of people in the truck. Many people were screaming and yelling. "I'm going to fall off the truck", "We are all going to die". And yet there were several others who had somehow managed to conquer their fears. Some were praying: "*Ya khoda, ya khoda, ya khoda. komak kon mara.*" ("Dear God, dear God, dear God, please save us.") Others were even singing, love songs to their fiancés, to their mothers, and others were just singing popular songs from singers like Ahmad Zaher and Sarah Ban.

The horrendous conditions did not get any better when we crossed into Iran. We knew we had crossed into Iran because we recognised the men as Balochi from the especially baggy pants they were wearing, the lighter colour of their skin, and the fact that they were speaking the Balochi language. At times, the pickups stopped at the gates of big buildings that seemed like huge garages, with high walls, open to the sky, with a small room at the top of the entrance where the smugglers gathered. We all jumped out, the smugglers came and counted us, and then they settled us in certain parts of the space. The floors were dirt, dirt that was so loose that if you stepped on it, a cloud of it would engulf your ankles, and yet we were forced to sit there. The sun beat down on us mercilessly. Hundreds of people were crushed in there together, struggling to find a comfortable place to lie down, and using their clothes to create some shade from the sun. The numbers increased every hour as more pickups and taxis arrived and disgorged their loads. There were no bathroom facilities and so we had to relieve ourselves in the very same spaces where we were trying to rest. And then there were times when guards would find someone in a corner, trying to go to the bathroom, and they would beat him and tell him he was dirtying the space for everyone else. It was especially humiliating for the women, who tried desperately to retain some sense of privacy. For all of us, even more difficult than the physical challenges, was the fact that we could feel our dignity being stripped away. Even when the smugglers offered us small pieces of *naan*, they threw them at us so that we had to fight over it as if we were dogs. We were being treated worse than animals and could see no relief in sight.

The only comfort for me had been the company of Hassan. We had managed to stay together throughout the past six days and that had given me some strength and hope. But I lost track of him when it was time for us to leave this space, where we had been locked up for nearly 24 hours. The new smugglers gathered up the 60 people in our group and distributed us into four taxis. Hassan and I were put into different cars. We did meet up, however, a few days later in Bam.

It took two days for us to reach Bam. It was a particularly terrifying place. The smuggler left us in a walled-in forest with very high reeds along a dried creek bed for two days and our only food was what we could pick from the date palms. At one point, I went out with another guy to find water. We had no success; we couldn't find any after walking far, so we returned because it was getting dark. When we returned, we found that the rest of the group had been traumatised. Two people had been taken from the group by armed men and they never came back. We had no idea who those armed men were and what they wanted. But their actions confirmed what we had heard about Bam, that it was a terrible part of the journey. Stories abounded about kidnappers taking people, cutting off their noses or ears, and using that as a way of persuading their families to pay a high ransom.

Then Hassan started taking control. Our group was shivering with fear. He had everybody huddle together in the shelter of the high reeds while he gathered the strongest of the men and had them pick up heavy sticks. They guarded the rest of us as we remained together in a tight circle. We stayed like that all night. None of us could sleep. I was the smallest so I remained in the very centre of the circle, drenched in sweat because I was so afraid.

The next day we just sat there, waiting for instructions or a message from our smuggler. At three in the afternoon, we could hear the sound of shooting in the distance. The police were shooting at another group of Afghans who had been hiding in a spot a few kilometres from us. The Afghans started running towards us with the police right behind them, and so the police soon discovered our group too. 12 people from our group were arrested while the rest of us were running away desperately. The forest had high walls surrounding it; we had to scale the walls and jump down to escape the shots of the police. It was in that spot that we found our smuggler who ordered us to follow him out of the forest; he wanted to get away from the police as much as we did. For three hours we ran and ran, with the sounds of shooting still resounding in the air around us. We never learned what happened to those 12 people. The rest of us gathered together and climbed into another taxi that the smuggler had arranged to continue our journey.

The topography of this part of Iran is very harsh, deserts and high mountains. Taxis and pickup trucks were of no use in the mountains of Iran which are bleak and inhospitable with their high peaks and paths covered in pebbles and small rocks. We hated this part of the journey; we had very little water and could only drink one sip at a time, conserving the little water we had because we had no idea how long the trip across a mountain would last. Most of us were wearing the only shoes we owned, sneakers and sandals completely unsuited to the terrain. Women had the most difficult time; some of them were pregnant or nursing their babies, holding the hands of toddlers, urging on their ageing parents and grandparents. But we were the fortunate ones, we were travelling in the summer; I have no idea how people survived this trip in the winter with its bitter cold, biting winds and high snow.

This part of the trip was so tough that we were relieved to see the taxis and pickups that would take us the last few hundred kilometres to Tehran. Of course, we had no idea at the time that we only had a few hundred more kilometres to go; we had absolutely no idea where we were. We had no GPS, no maps, and no communication with anyone to let us know where we were and how much longer our suffering would continue. It was hard to keep up our morale but there was no time to reflect, no time for depression, no time for questioning what we had done. Our only thoughts were to arrive somewhere safe and begin planning for new lives.

But I had one more challenge before I could get to Tehran. The very last part of the journey was on an Iranian inter-city bus. The smuggler took me with four other people and put us into the luggage compartment. That didn't seem too bad at first but it quickly got worse.

He pushed us into a very small, closed compartment at the very front of the luggage hold.

We had to crawl in and stay in that position for the next 14 hours. But the very worst, after we crawled in, was that the cover was put back in and screwed into place from the outside. It was terrifying. The five of us had been given three big bottles of water, they were frozen when the smuggler handed them to us but within minutes they were boiling hot. We could hardly breathe, we were drenched in sweat, and had to do everything we could not to panic completely. We were aware the entire time that just inches above our heads were Iranian passengers sitting comfortably, who had no idea of the hell beneath them. The trip lasted from 1 am until 3 pm. When we reached the bus stop in Tehran, the passengers all got off but we were still locked up in the compartment and had no idea what would happen next. After a short delay, the bus took off again and drove to an isolated spot where we were finally released and put into a waiting taxi that had been arranged by the smuggler.

I had reached my destination, Tehran. In my mind at that moment, I had reached the end of my journey. But I was wrong; an even longer journey was waiting for me.

Chapter 4
In Tehran

Kabul, Tehran, Istanbul, Athens, Helsinki. These are the big cities that have shaped my life these past few years. All of them have had a big influence on the young boy from a tiny village in a far-away province in a country that is trapped in violence and in many ways has not yet caught up with the twenty-first century. Right now, I'm sitting in a café in Athens, a hot summer day, playing chess with Dove, an American guy who has become a very good friend. We sit facing the Acropolis as we remember the details of my past. Athens for me is a place that I am very familiar with; I spent eight months here living in a shelter for unaccompanied minors, roaming the streets with my friends, getting used to being in Europe, and taking the first steps towards my education in this part of the world. It has left a strong mark on me, I still have very good friends here, I learned to play chess and backgammon here, I read *Harry Potter*, my first book in English here, and it was here that I met my mother.

I will leave in three weeks for Helsinki. I was sent to Finland a year ago from Athens under family reunification because my brother Alijan lives there. I am a student at the International School of Helsinki and I will be in the ninth grade this fall. I have become accustomed to a society very different from that of Greece, but I love Helsinki. I love the summer weather, the saunas, the very friendly and polite culture, a culture that observes all the rules that make life easy and calm, a culture that places a great value on education at all levels.

But my first big city was Tehran. The difficult journey, mountains and deserts, taxis and pickup trucks, smuggler after smuggler, the constant hunger and thirst, the looming fear of violence or of being left behind, was over.

As soon as I got out of the bus, the smuggler blindfolded me and Hassan and put us in a taxi with another Afghan guy for a three-hour trip. At the end, the taxi stopped in the middle of nowhere, with nothing in sight except dirt in the air from the smokestacks of factories in the distance. Those factories were most likely producing bricks and plaster and other building materials for the construction industry in Tehran. The place was desolate and desperately hot, with no trees and with heavy dust in the air that filled our noses and made it difficult to breathe. After we got out of the taxi, we took off our blindfolds and then we had to climb a steep hill, until we reached an old, dilapidated compound, probably an old stable. A group of smugglers came out to meet us. One of the smugglers was holding a long sword in his hands as he pushed us first into a small room where all the other smugglers were hanging out. From there we were forced into a big room where there were hundreds of Afghans, and we were shocked since the place had seemed completely empty when we first arrived. Once we were inside that crowded room, the guy with the sword locked the door from the outside, a door made of tightly fitted bars, just like bars in a jail cell. Obviously, this place was meant to be hidden from the authorities, which is the reason it had looked so abandoned at first and why they took such precautions with keeping us locked inside this room in the middle of nowhere.

We tried to figure out exactly what kind of place this was. The jail-like door felt ominous. Worse was the fact that the guy with the sword stood at the door and kept pushing the sword through the bars to keep away the crowds who kept pressing against the door.

As soon as we entered the room, we were surrounded by a crowd. "Do you have any cigarettes? Any opium? Marijuana?" The people looked bedraggled and desperate, with eyes that seemed to have lost all hope. We heard terrible stories of people who had no one to pay the smuggler for their release, of others who were waiting for months for the money to come through, and of others who had to go to work for the smugglers to pay off their debt. Any happiness we felt at being near Tehran evaporated in the fetid atmosphere.

There was another guy standing at the door and he called out my group since we were the most recent arrivals. He called us up according to our smuggling group name; my group at this point was called 'Potato' but I, as all the others, had also been in groups like 'Pomegranate', 'Tomato', 'Cucumber'. It got to the point that it was hard to remember what fruit we were at any time.

At this point, one of the smugglers gave me a phone and yelled at me, "Call anyone you know who can pay for your trip." The only thing I could think of was to call Omid, the Afghan who had stayed with us in Baghlan the previous year after being deported from Iran. His was the only number I had on my phone other than my brother's, so I called him and asked if he could help me. I was very nervous and my hands were shaking, all my hope of escaping this awful place lay in his agreeing to help me. Fortunately, he said yes. I became very happy when I heard his answer because this meant that I would be able to avoid the fate of those people who couldn't pay. So, Omid set about getting the money and sending it so that they would let me go.

I was a lucky one, to be able to be released from that room. I shouldn't really call it a room, since it really was a combination of a stable and a jail cell. The room held many, many people, and there was no space for us to sit or lie down. There were no bathrooms, so we just used the corners of the room. Food was passed through the bars of the door and consisted of just a small piece of bread. We were all men; I have no idea where the women were being kept.

To my surprise, my friend Hassan stayed there with me, even after he had the ability to leave. Somehow, he had managed to get released in just about an hour. But he was still hanging around.

"Hassan," I asked, "what are you doing here? I thought your money already came through and you could leave."

"I'm waiting for you," was his reply.

"No, Hassan, leave now. Get out of this place."

Those were my words but I was hoping he would stay and not leave me alone.

His answer touched me deeply. He told me that he was waiting for my money to come through so we could leave together. And if it didn't come through, he would help me to find enough money to get released.

Finally, after the money transfer from Omid reached the smugglers, I was released from the room. Hassan and I were put into a taxi driven by a guy who was working with the smugglers. He asked us for the fare ahead of time but since we had no money, he searched us and grabbed everything that we still had. He ended up taking my backpack and my phone; he held on to them until the end of the trip to be sure that he would be paid. Then he blindfolded us at the beginning of the trip so we wouldn't be able to describe the location of the place where we had been held. He started off for the address I had given him. After about ten minutes, he told us we could remove the blindfolds. It took us about three hours to get to Omid's house.

This taxi trip was remarkable for a number of reasons. First of all, we felt free. But most of all, we were once again, after 13 long days and nights, seeing normal life again. We couldn't believe that the crazy pickup drives and harsh walks across mountains were over. Now we could look out the windows and see regular life as we drove through the outskirts of Tehran, other cars on the road, people walking on the sidewalks, shops, restaurants, mosques, parks. No words can express the relief we felt.

We also noticed the differences between Iran and Afghanistan. Men walked the streets in jeans instead of traditional Afghani dress, women also were on the streets, covered in scarves but not burkas, the streets were clean, houses were made of concrete and plaster and not mudbrick. There were traffic lights, which are non-existent in the small towns of Afghanistan, different hairstyles, neon lights, children playing on the sidewalks instead of begging or polishing shoes. There were no cows or horses or donkeys on the streets.

But we felt a connection with the scene around us when we noticed some people practising the familiar Shiite rituals.

It was the holy month of *Muharram* and people were in the streets beating drums, beating their chests with their arms, listening and following the beat of the dirge being chanted.

After this drive that was so fascinating for us, we finally reached Omid's house. He came out and paid the taxi driver. The driver gave me back my phone and my backpack. Finally, I was free. I was so happy when I was greeted by Omid and his family and when I entered his apartment, which was like heaven after everything I had suffered the past 13 days. But I was terribly embarrassed by my condition, imagine after 13 days, no shower, intense sweat, sleeping in the dirt and other filthy places, never taking my shoes off. My skin was covered in thick layers of dirt that would take weeks to finally be scraped away. Thick calluses covered my feet; I needed to use a knife to begin to remove them. I knew that my body had a stench to it, and even after a week or two of showers, I could still sense that smell.

But on that first day with them, I took probably the most wonderful shower of my life and then they helped me soak my feet in warm, salty water. That was followed by the most delicious meal of my life, *Shorbah*, a typical Afghani soup.

Although these were distant relatives, I think cousins of my grandfather, they treated me so kindly, as if I were their son. Of course, Omid had stayed with my family for three months the previous year after he had been deported back to Afghanistan and I got to know him pretty well. But little did I imagine then how important a role he would play in my life. His family treated me so well at a time I was so vulnerable and fragile; their relatives came by to meet me even though I was embarrassed because I was in such a rough state.

Hassan stayed with us for the first night and was able to shower and get cleaned up and fed a healthy meal. Then he left, saying that he had an aunt in Tehran and that he would stay with her. I would meet up with him ten months later in Tehran, and would become distraught then at the condition I would find him in.

I ended up staying with Omid's family for three months. I never got over feeling awkward there. From the first moment I entered the house, when the sisters and sisters-in-law peeked out the window at me, I was aware that, according to our customs, it was not normal for a boy my age to be in a home with young women who were not close relatives. I felt that especially with their daughter, who was the same age as me. On days that I didn't go to work, I would lock myself in my room so that I wouldn't disturb their daughter and put all of us in an uncomfortable situation.

Two days after I arrived, I went with Omid's brother to a brick factory where he worked in an important role; I was given the place of an absent employee. I worked on an assembly line where I had to sort out the bricks before they went into the kiln. This was my first day of work in Iran and it was a very difficult day. In the first place, I couldn't speak Farsi and all the other workers made fun of my accent since my language was Dari, closely related to Farsi but with some differences in vocabulary and pronunciation. They also kept laughing when I couldn't use the gloves properly and my fingers gave out after the first few hours. The work was too hard for me, but I was desperate to make money to pay back Omid for what he gave to the smuggler. At the end of the day the boss told me that I was too young and that I couldn't come back the next day. I finished my shift and went back home, utterly exhausted. But I am such a proud person that I was ashamed when I had to let the family know how hard the day had been. I stayed home with the family for the next week as they tried to find a job for me. I did work a few days, picking cucumbers, squash, tomatoes, and eggplant with Omid's mother. Since this was considered women's work, the pay was very little and so I knew I had to find something more.

After one week, I went with Omid to the construction site where he worked. He worked for a building contractor who had just won a contract to construct roads in an immense dairy farm. The job I was assigned was to move bags of cement mix from their storage place to the cement mixer and then shovel the mix in. I was also given the task of making small drainage channels at the sides of the road after the concrete had been poured. I was not strong enough; the cement mix bags were very heavy and I could barely lift the wheelbarrow. So, they told me that I couldn't continue working there. I pleaded with them, since I needed the money desperately. Finally, they agreed to keep me, but they would only give me half the normal salary. For me, though, this was a good salary and so I continued working there for the next three months.

The days at work were unbearable for me. The manager was an Afghan, so at first, I had expected he would treat me well. But he was cruel to me from the very beginning. He called me names and beat me if I didn't understand what he wanted. What was even more shocking to me was that the other workers, all of them Afghans, joined in with him and bullied me and did nothing to help me. The manager took advantage of me in other ways too, by forcing me to work on another project for five more hours after the eight hours of work I had already done for him that day. I was constantly in a state of anxiety and felt trapped and couldn't see any way out of that situation.

On the other hand, the one thing I could look forward to was returning to Omid's family at the end of each day. I rode to and from work on the back of Omid's motorbike. And when I returned home each night, the family had made a good dinner for me, had washed my clothes, and had warm water ready for my shower. I was overwhelmed by their kindness and generosity and felt embarrassed that I was so needy.

After three months, the construction at the site was finished and so I was out of a job. I had saved some money but it was just enough to pay them back. And I was in terrible shape; I had no phone with internet access to be in touch with my brothers in Afghanistan, my clothes were in tatters, my shoes falling apart. Then the family showed once again their kind spirits; they told me to use the money I had earned to go and buy a phone and some new clothes. I went shopping and bought my first smartphone and some new clothes and a new pair of Adidas. I had a little money left and I gave it to them to begin to pay back what I owed them.

I continued to stay with this family until one of my cousins came to take me to Isfahan to live with my aunt. But I had heard that this cousin was a drug addict and also Isfahan was far from Tehran and it would be a dangerous journey for me since I had no papers. My cousin kept insisting but I didn't trust him and didn't want to relive my bus experience. But he did do something that helped me in the next steps of my life. At one time in the past, he had worked in a sewing factory in Tehran and now he learned that they needed a helper, so he introduced me to the boss, who hired me for that position.

And so I moved out of the house of Omid's family and started living and working in the sewing factory which produced women's clothes. Moving out was not completely easy. There is a police force in Iran called *Afghani Begir*, which means the 'Catching Afghans' force. I needed to take a long bus ride to get from the part of the city where Omid's family lived (a village called Mohammadabad in Peshwa Varamin, an area almost completely populated by Afghans) to the part of the city where the sewing factory was located, Tajrish, a very prosperous and beautiful area in the outskirts of the city, in the foothills of the mountains, where very wealthy and successful people built their homes. I had to plan carefully so that I went at a time when I was less likely to be caught. I left the house at 7 pm, hoping that the police would not be around, since the workday was over. Being on the bus, filled with Iranians and alone after being with Omid's family for so long, made me feel very isolated and lonely. People were going about their business, many of them well dressed and professional. I knew they were all living lives very different from mine. It made me feel that I was alive but not really living. I began to long for a different kind of life but I had no idea how I could ever attain that.

I arrived at the factory at 9 pm. There were several people around since the boss always stayed late and since there were two workers who lived in the factory, as I would. In the beginning, I started out just helping, picking up scraps of fabric and doing odd jobs. I was responsible for chalk-marking patterns onto fabric and holding down the fabric while it was cut. The guy I worked with, who did the cutting, actually was uneducated and knew no math, so I also helped out with all the measurements and calculations. I worked 16 hours per day and received half the salary of the other workers, and the boss never even really paid me and just gave me a very little amount of money at the end of each week, just enough so I didn't starve to death.

There was another section in the factory; it was there that the cut fabric was sewn into fancy dresses. I was intrigued by that work and so I would go over there at random times of the day and start to learn the process of stitching garments from one of the workers named Jawad. He was happy to have me there because I turned out to be useful for him and so he started giving me a little money each week out of his own wages. I was thinking of my future, that if I stayed on the other side, I would always be a helper and a cleaner. But if I learned to sew, I could see a future for myself, eventually opening my own shop. So, I went to the manager and told him I didn't want to work on the first side anymore; he told me that I couldn't leave unless I could find someone to take my place. And so I faced one of my first ethical challenges, and still to this day I feel guilty about it. I found another Afghan guy to replace me, and that enabled me to quit that job and go to work for Jawad in the sewing section. Before I started working with him, he could make 10–12 dresses a day but with me there, he could make about 20. I was happy with what he agreed to pay me and also because he treated me like a human being with dignity. I was also happy that I was learning a skill that could help me in the future. And even more, he paid me a fairly generous amount of money and he was very honest and paid me each week.

One of the reasons he hired me was that I had learned the process so quickly; what took other workers two or three years to learn, I learned in just a few months. I was beginning to see the value of education and how it could help me move forward. I was grateful for the education I had received in my village because it gave me skills and strategies I could apply in this job, which helped me gain the approval and goodwill of Jawad. A lot of the sewing and accounting depended on the ability with math, and I was given the job of calculating how many dresses were made each day and what that meant for the bottom line.

I also lived in the factory, sleeping most nights underneath the cutting table, on top of and surrounded by huge bolts of fabrics. Sometimes people would bring me food but most days I cooked small meals by myself. I bought the food at a supermarket located just 50 metres from the factory. It was very dangerous for me to go out; I had to avoid the police or face imprisonment or deportation. So, I would run to the market and bring a few groceries back with me. I also always had to be vigilant in the factory because the police would stage raids every once in a while, and I didn't want to be caught.

At the same time, the factory was falling apart; the boss couldn't pay his workers and his suppliers. In fact, he continued to cheat me out of my money, both during the four months I worked on his side of the factory and afterwards when I moved to the other side to work with Jawad. I continued to meet with him to ask for my money. I tried to make him realise that I needed it, by referring to the needs of my family in Afghanistan and to my sick grandmother. Each time we met, he was very soft-spoken and polite. And he always promised that he would pay me the money. But nothing ever happened and I have lost that money forever.

I knew that it was time to find another job. But there was a big question for me, how could I do that?

I was trying to figure out what to do; after living in constant fear and with the troubles with my job, I felt that I needed to make a change. But I still needed to pay back Omid and his family for their payment to my smuggler. Suddenly, I received calls from two of my brothers, Jawad in Afghanistan and Alijan in Finland. My brother Alijan wanted me to come to Finland to be with him and my brother Jawad agreed with him that that's what I should do. They both decided to send money to me for the trip. I had managed to save up some money from my sewing job, so all of a sudden, I had the opportunity to leave, and I could pay back my loan, buy a good backpack, and have money for a smuggler. My brother Alijan had a Finnish friend who was volunteering in Lesvos and he told me to try to get there while she was still there.

For the first time in my journey, I had a plan for the future.

So, I went back to Omid and his family and asked them how I could find a smuggler to get me to Europe. There were many questions in their minds. Omid, who was just a few years older than I was, kept telling me I shouldn't go to Europe because I was too young. It made me feel that they still thought that I was a kid, but of course, even though I was still just 13, I felt old inside.

I had survived deserts and mountains, cramped trucks and taxis, bus compartments, hunger and thirst and cold and heat. I had worked in construction, I had dealt with sleazy bosses, and learned a trade. How many other 13-year-olds have these experiences? So, I might have been still young but my experiences made me feel old.

After long conversations, the family agreed to find a smuggler for me. This was a week before I left Tehran. I needed to wait until Friday to make my preparations because the police are not out on Fridays. On Friday, I went into the centre of the city and bought a backpack, some almonds and raisins and walnuts. I also changed some money from Iranian tomans into American dollars. I had saved the money I got paid from my job on the bank card of Jawad, the guy I sewed with, so I went to an ATM and withdrew that money. That might sound crazy, that I trusted my pay with him but for Afghans without visas in Iran, it is a necessity to have their money in accounts under the name of an Iranian citizen because the nearly two million Afghans cannot have bank accounts in their own names. That also means that they can't buy property or cars under their own names but must entrust their money to their Iranian friends who can do those things legally.

During these last days in Tehran, I called people I had become friends with to say goodbye to them. One of the people I called was my friend Hassan, Hassan who had saved all of us on the pickup and who had been so loyal to me that he waited for me to leave for Tehran. He told me where he lived and I went to see him. I was shocked. The place he was living was filthy, one room with maybe ten other Afghans. They all worked on farms, picking lettuce. My stomach turned at the dirt and the stench in the room. But even more upsetting was the sight of Hassan himself. I had looked up to him so much. He had been so strong, so powerful, and so good. Now he was a shadow of that earlier Hassan, pale, skinny, his hair long and stringy. It was clear that they were all using drugs in that place. In fact, they had two little gas burners, one was used for cooking and the other for processing the opium they used. Hassan, ever generous, ran to get food to make chicken *Shorbah* but I could hardly eat it, sitting on the floor in this hovel. After a few bites, I said I had to leave. Hassan urged me to continue eating; in some ways, I was being rude by asking to leave before the meal was over. But I had to leave to finish the errands I needed to do. He understood and then took me outside, called a taxi for me, and we said goodbyes filled with emotion.

"Hassan," I said. "What's going on here?"

"What do you mean?"

"I saw everything. All these drugs. You are better than this. You deserve more."

He muttered a couple of things but he really had no answer. I left with a very heavy heart. Here I was headed to Europe, and he, with an almost hopeless future in front of him. I wished with all my heart that I could have done something to help him since he had helped me so much on my journey. But I could barely take care of myself, let alone a guy in his situation. I felt intense sadness as I gave him a last hug. I had no idea if we would ever see each other again.

A day or two later, it was time for me to leave. I received a phone call one night informing me that I would leave the next day. I had to go to a place called *Meydan Azadi*, a big landmark in Tehran. I needed to be there at 1 pm. I said goodbye to the family. One more time I had to say goodbye to a family, this time a family that had cared for me as if I were their own son. All memories of leaving my own family in Afghanistan came back to me and I remembered my last words to my sister and my brothers. These memories made me realise how mature I had become, very different from the child who had left my village almost a year ago. I was marked deeply by all my experiences; I hoped that I would have the strength for the next few days which surely would be difficult ones for me.

Chapter 5
Leaving Tehran

I took a taxi to *Meydan Azadi*. The taxi driver saw my backpack and asked me where I was travelling to. I couldn't let him know the truth, so I told him I was headed to Syria to fight against ISIS. This was easy for him to believe because Iran had a pattern of sending young Afghan men to Syria to fight. It was common for the Iranian Revolutionary Guard to stage raids, either on the streets of Tehran or in factories, both places that were likely to have groups of young Afghans. The Afghans would be rounded up and taken to a police station and given a choice, either immediate deportation to Afghanistan or the option to go and fight in Syria. Most chose to go to Syria; they had little understanding of what the war was about and found the prospect of the salary they would receive as soldiers very attractive.

So that was the story I told the taxi driver so that he wouldn't take me to the police. He wanted to show his gratitude for my patriotism, so he didn't charge me for the taxi ride.

When I arrived at *Meydan Azadi*, I called the smuggler and he asked me where I was. I didn't know the area so I described where I was. He told me to walk towards a big park I could see in front of me, and then to keep walking through it. I followed his directions and started walking through the park, but I was filled with panic, thinking that I was very vulnerable and could be caught by the police very easily. How awful would that be, just as I was about to leave Iran and escape the grasp of the police, to be apprehended and taken to the police station. As I passed a thick group of trees, however, I heard someone call my name. I approached him, relieved to have escaped the police. I saw small groups of people, about twenty in all, scattered around. It didn't seem that they were together but it turned out that they were all smugglers waiting for the people they were going to smuggle. They were speaking several languages and I couldn't understand them. Once more I was put in a situation where I was among people I didn't know, couldn't understand, and who seemed threatening to me. I was scared and started shaking. But by now I knew Farsi well and that turned out to be a common language, and that made me feel more comfortable, despite the fact that I was talking to men whose job was trafficking human beings. They brought me some bread and even bought me a meal of rice and meat. While I was eating, we even chatted.

This situation with the smugglers showed how much I had learned and how much I had matured since my experiences with smugglers in the previous year. I understood what was going on and that knowledge made me feel a little more secure. I didn't dare speak calmly with the smugglers when I left Afghanistan. But these smugglers in Tehran were different, not as violent or threatening as those earlier ones in Iran had been. And my experiences had taught me that some conversation with them, some attempt to connect at a human level, could bring a little bit of protection to me. That was something that I needed acutely, now that I no longer had Hassan with me.

So, I waited there with the smugglers for two or three hours until more people arrived. Afghans were coming from all over Iran; Shiraz, Zaidan, Mashhad. When they arrived, they looked for the smugglers they had been in contact with. There were four taxis standing by and we were put in groups and then put in individual taxis. Because we had to ride through the city, we did not want to arouse any suspicion in the police and so the taxis were not overcrowded. Only about eight of us were allotted to each taxi. The rear seats, though, had been removed and five people sat on the floor back there, two sat upfront with the driver, and I was put into the trunk. I loved being in the trunk this time, even though it felt a little like being buried alive. I was alone and could stretch out and nap the whole time.

After four or five hours, the driver asked me to come up front to the back of the taxi and another guy was placed into the trunk. This new position was not as good for me as the trunk; there were five of us and we kept continuously jostling each other in an attempt to find a comfortable position.

The four taxis travelled together in a group. Generally, the ride was a smooth one along the highway and we passed the time listening to Kurdish songs on a CD but there were spots where we had to go onto rough back roads to avoid police checkpoints. There were also several checkpoints we went through with no problem; the drivers said something to the police and probably handed them some money, and we went through without trouble. At first, those spots really scared me, I expected that I would be arrested and either put in jail, or sent back to Afghanistan, or sent to Syria. But everything

74

worked smoothly and we arrived in Urmia, a city in western Iran, after a trip of about ten hours.

As we entered the city, the smugglers began transferring passengers one by one into other new taxis that were waiting at specific spots. There was a taxi waiting for me; a new smuggler also was waiting for me there. He was accompanied by five of his friends, all Iranian, who spoke only Kurdish, and they blasted Kurdish music as we drove through the outskirts of the city. Each of these guys was in his 20s and each had a very long beard. Now I felt real fear. Who were they? Fighters from ISIS? It was 1 am and completely dark outside. What would happen to me? I was completely alone. What would they do to me?

They could kill me and drop my body somewhere and no one would ever know. They drove me for an hour, away from the city, into a huge forest. I couldn't say even one word to them because I was paralysed by fear. The smuggler then took me to a building inside a big garden, completely isolated with nothing else in sight. We all entered the building and to my surprise, they let me join in with them to eat the dinner they prepared. After dinner, I withdrew to a side of the room, hoping to escape their attention. But they then sat in a circle in the middle of the room and started smoking a hookah. They asked me if I wanted to join them: "Hey, Afghan. *Qelion mikashi?*" ("Do you smoke hookah?") I was trying to feel comfortable with them and I thought that it would help if I joined them. Now that I was able to speak to them, by talking about the flavours, I was able to have a common experience with them and I hoped that that would win me their sympathy. This was one thing my journey had taught me, that if you are hoping to find sympathy from someone, find a common human experience.

The night went on and I slept in one room in a bed by myself. I was still afraid, being in such an isolated place with people I didn't know, so I tried to stay awake but the exhaustion from the journey and the emotions were too much and I fell deeply asleep. It was a fitful sleep; I kept waking up to see if I was still safe. In the morning, I had a hearty breakfast of peaches and apricots and cherries along with an omelette. After we ate, I nervously asked the smuggler when I would leave for Turkey and he told me he didn't know. The large numbers of refugees had dwindled and they needed to wait for enough Afghans to arrive there to make the trip to Turkey feasible.

The smuggler and his friends then went away and left me all alone in that place until the next day. I was filled with panic and my imagination made me consider all the terrible things that could happen to me. Then he showed up the next day with his car and took me with him to his house in a nearby village. I stayed there with him and his family for several days. He took me into the village and went for long walks with me. There were no police in that small town and for the first time since I entered Iran, I felt safe. I also realised from some of the things he said to me that one reason he was treating me so well was that he was hoping for me to recruit other refugees for him once I reached Turkey.

Finally, it was time to leave. After several days, a taxi arrived at his house to pick me up. The taxi driver drove me for a while until we arrived at another taxi that was waiting for me. Big difference this time, since I was the only passenger and I even sat in the front seat with the driver and he told me to put on my seatbelt. But this driver was scary in his own way; he drove very fast and I was afraid of crashing.

Then I arrived at a small village close to the mountains that formed the border between Iran and Turkey. The taxi driver dropped me off at a house in the village and told me to run into the house without letting anyone see me. A man was waiting for me there; he lived there with his wife and children. He took me into the house and I sat down in the living room. He grabbed my backpack and asked, "What do you have there?" I told him that I just had clothes and some dried fruit. Without another word, he searched my backpack and took half of the fruit, telling me that what was left was enough for me, that I didn't need to eat too much. But then I asked and he let me take a shower and then he led me to the bedroom where I could take a nap. After I settled into the bed, I heard him lock the room from the outside and once more I began to panic. I was able to fall asleep because I was so drained but when I woke up, I realised that I couldn't open the door.

There was a small window in the room and I stood up and looked out of it. His daughter, a skinny dark scraggly little girl, was outside and saw me and started shouting, "Afghan, Afghan."

The man came running up and said, "Fucking Afghan, put your head back inside. You want the police to come and arrest me?"

All I could think was that I wished that the situation was reversed and he was in a vulnerable position in Afghanistan and I could pay him back for the way he was treating me.

I was at this house until 9 pm. When it got dark, this guy drove me to a place about ten minutes away, the foothills of the mountains that form the border between Iran and Turkey.

He let me out of the car and told me to run as fast as I could down the hill. As I ran, I heard someone calling to me, "*Afghan, bia inja.*" ("*Afghan*, come here.") I got closer and I could see a big group of people, about a hundred, Uzbeks, Pakistanis, Pashtuns but no one else who could speak Farsi. It was the new smuggler who had been calling me; he had been waiting for me and was relieved to recognise me because I could understand his Farsi. The smuggler forced us to cross the highway to get to the hills. It was dark but there was some traffic so we had to find a time when no cars were coming, in order to cross without being seen. There were several people who had trouble walking or running but the smuggler beat them to force them to move quickly. It took a number of attempts for all of us to make it across the road safely but finally, we did it.

When we got to the hills, we all had to run. I remembered the time when I had to cross from Afghanistan into Iran and felt like I had ended up in the same situation again. The difficulty of running up a mountain, the fear of your foot slipping and you falling over the side into the abyss, the cold, the thirst. We ran for a few hours, until about 1 am, and then we reached a point where we could see the border. A dirt road ran along with it but it was lined with barbed wire, and we could see police cars travelling at high speeds down that road. We knew that we would not be able to pass across the road without being seen, so we just sat on the peak and waited there while the smuggler called other smugglers to find a safe route. In the background, the sound of gunfire could be heard. We started climbing down the side of the mountain, a few steps at a time, then crouching down and hiding before we regained the courage to start moving again. I was walking at the front of the group with the smuggler since I could speak Farsi. I kept walking with him even when my leg was hurt by stones rolling down the mountain.

Chapter 6
Into Turkey

Finally, at 5:30 am we reached the road, the border. We waited until the cars had passed and then the smuggler yelled at us to cross. We all ran as fast as we could and made it across the border. There were some injuries from the barbed wire and we could hear police shooting but we kept running, made it across the road, and started up the mountains on the Turkish side. Luckily, we were able to escape the Iranian police.

The trip over the mountains took us one day, but we felt safe from the police and so we didn't have to run. It was not an easy trip; the mountain side was covered by boulders and immense rocks, and we had to jump from rock to rock. Many people fell and were injured, and most people's legs were covered in blood, and their shoes had been torn to pieces. It also was very very hot and there was no water. My lips were stuck together because they were so dry. There were many times I fell and could not get up because I was so thirsty and weak. Once I saw a guy who had a little bit of water and I asked him if he would give me one sip but he grabbed the bottle of water and turned away from me and said, "No, I will die if I give you this water. This is the only water I have left and I don't know how long this journey will take us."

At last, the smuggler brought me half of a small bottle of water and said, "This is the only water that I will give you and the journey will take us five more hours." The water revived me and we continued walking. Five hours later, we were very happy to reach level ground.

Once we were out of the mountains, we faced a large expanse of desert, with the sun beating down mercilessly. We were desperately looking for shade but there were no trees around and we could not find any way to avoid the sun. But all of a sudden, we saw in front of us several blankets on the ground next to three vans, covered with bottles of water and packages of cookies for sale. As soon as we caught sight of them, we all ran to buy what we could so that we were finally able to eat and drink and recover from our difficult journey over the mountain.

Once we all had our water and cookies, the smugglers pushed us into the vans. Again, I had to relive an experience; these vans were as crowded as the pickup trucks I had ridden a year earlier. We were driven through a desert for two hours until we arrived at a small village, the first Turkish village we had seen.

To an ordinary tourist, this village might look like any other little settlement in a remote area in Turkey. To smugglers and to the villagers, it had become a centre of their business, a way to make more money than they ever could with their customary farming, but to refugees it was hell. There were those of us who were lucky were able to leave after a day or two but there were others who languished there for years.

In the village, the driver would stop the van every few minutes and tell one person to get off, and there would be another smuggler waiting for him there. The smuggler who picked me up took me to a house with a yard. One side of the yard was space for his family but on the other side, there were two connected rooms, each with one door and a tiny window placed high on the door. The smuggler opened one of the doors and pushed me in. The room I entered was jammed full with a hundred Pakistanis. I could hear a voice from the other side saying in Farsi, "Afghan, come over to this room. We just had a fight with those Pakistanis and they might kill you." So, I crossed over into the second room. A big shock. A hundred Afghans were there, packed in. No space for me. They were all sitting and standing on top of each other. I learned that there were people who had been there for several years, people who hadn't had money to give the smugglers. They had made an agreement with the smuggler to work for him to pay off their debt. Their job was to cook and clean inside the room but the food was awful and I couldn't bear to eat it, even though I was so hungry.

There was no water, no bathroom.

The agreement between Omid's family in Tehran and the smuggler was that he would be paid only when I reached Turkey. Now that I was there, I was instructed to call the family and give them an account number to deposit the money. But I had no SIM card to be able to call them. The smugglers, however, sold SIM cards at a price that was ten times normal. I had no choice so I bought the SIM card but the price of the internet was exorbitant and I couldn't afford that. I could call within Turkey, though, so I called an Afghan friend in Istanbul. His name was Islam and he had been my classmate in Baghlan. I had found him on Facebook when I was in Iran and connected with him and told him that I would try to see him when I got to Turkey. He was the only one I knew in Turkey at that time, so I called him and asked him if he could help. He was able to send me a few gigabytes of internet and 100 minutes of talking time for countries outside Turkey. He saved my life. I was able to connect with the family in Tehran, so they could pay the smuggler, and I was even able to call my family in Afghanistan. I also was able to help other refugees in the room; I let them use my minutes and my gigabytes so they could be in touch with their relatives too.

That was one way I survived this journey, a journey that could easily strip away all dignity from a human being. By giving away the gigabytes I didn't use, I was able to help others who were in need. That made me feel like a good person again, like a human being who could act and make decisions on my own. I had learned this big lesson from Hassan.

The night passed and at ten the next morning, the smuggler started reading out the names of the people who had paid. There was a bus waiting outside and those whose names were called could go out and get onto it. Once again, there was immense crowding but great relief that we were out of that house and also my own great relief that I was riding up above, and not in the luggage compartment.

It took us 30 hours to get to Istanbul. There were guys who would enter the bus at intervals during the day to sell Pepsi and pancakes and other food. I had no money left but I was starving. I told some guys standing around me to distract one of the food-sellers and that gave me the opportunity to steal three pancakes and one Pepsi. I am embarrassed even now to write about that. I feel shame for what I did. But the hunger overwhelmed me and caused me to act in a way that I had never acted before that or since that.

Finally, we arrived at the bus terminal and we all got off the bus. I just stood there; I had no idea what to do. The other people and the bus driver all just left and went off in different directions, as if they knew exactly what to do and where to go. But I just continued to stand there and wonder what my next step should be.

I also was completely disoriented. This was my first time in a city where I didn't know the language, where women were walking around with short skirts and without veils, and where men were wearing shorts. And the city scared me. I felt more fear there than in the mountains and deserts of my journey. What if I made a wrong step? What if I went in the wrong direction?

I started walking up and down the station and then I had the idea to call the smuggler from Tehran; we had told him that I wanted to go to Greece, not just Turkey. He gave me a Turkish phone number to call, a number for an Afghan smuggler who would come and pick me up. I called that guy and he told me to take a taxi, and to give my phone to the taxi driver so he could explain where to take me. When I reached that place, there was a house with an Afghan family staying there; they were also trying to get to Greece.

That house was in the Zeytinburnu area. I was free there; I could go out, go for walks, and that family was good to me. There was food; I ate well for the three days I was there after so many days of being hungry. The family had kids so I had someone to play with.

On the third day, the smuggler called me and said, "You will start your journey to Greece tonight, so get ready." He came and picked me up at about seven in the afternoon and took me to a park farther out from the city. He told me to get out and wait there and that a van would come to pick me up. If it didn't come, my instructions were to call him back. I told him that I couldn't do that because I had followed the advice of that family and had already wrapped my phone very tightly and carefully in plastic and duct tape to protect it for the trip across the sea. But he told me that I needed to unwrap it so I could call him if I needed to. And he told me not to worry about my phone getting wet on the trip; we were travelling on a very safe and comfortable boat so there would be no problem.

And so I got out and started my wait. I soon realised that other people were also being dropped off there. By the end of the evening, there were about 30 of us standing there waiting for the van. But it never came. We all finally realised that it wasn't coming and so we each started calling our smugglers for them to come and get us.

My smuggler came and took me to his house in the Aksaray area. The next night at 7 pm, he took me to buy a life jacket. I had never heard of such a thing so I had no way of checking to see if it was good. As soon as he bought it, he stuffed it into my backpack and told me to keep it hidden so that the police wouldn't see it and understand what the situation was. He then put me into a taxi and gave directions to the driver. After about 20 minutes, the taxi driver stopped and told me to get out. As soon as I did, a guy tapped my arm and told me to follow him but to stay a distance away from him so we wouldn't be spotted. I followed him for 10 or 15 minutes, through narrow alleyways of the city, until we reached a small van parked on the side of the road in a place hidden from view.

I got into the van which was already jam-packed with about 40 other people. We travelled nearly six hours until we reached a place near Aivali on the Turkish coast. When we arrived, the van driver pushed us out of the van. We all had to run for one hour until we reached the water where there was another group of 20 people waiting for us; some of them had been waiting in that spot for several days. We joined the other group and then I saw two smugglers filling a rubber boat with air. I was surprised when I saw that boat because I was expecting a real boat and not a rubber dinghy. None of us wanted to go by that kind of a boat. People were sobbing and frightened. One of the smugglers tried to calm everyone down but the other smuggler pointed a gun at us and forced us on. We all got on the boat; there were 60 of us on a boat that should have fit at most 20 people. There was no captain and none of us knew how to operate a boat.

The smuggler pointed his gun at one guy and said that he would be the captain. We were men, women, and many children, and most of us did not know how to swim, including me. For us, this was a terrifying experience, one of the most intense experiences of our lives, but it was not just our experience and story, it is the story of all of those who crossed the Aegean in this place. And it was difficult but, in many ways, not as difficult as all the mountains and deserts and car trunks and luggage compartments we had faced in the earlier part of our journey. If we drowned in the ocean, we would suffer for some moments and then it would be over; the suffering in the mountains and deserts had lasted for days and days.

We had been in the boat for three hours in the middle of the sea with Turkey behind us and Greece in front of us. The guy who had been appointed as captain actually figured out how to run the boat and we felt calm; some people were even taking selfies, celebrating the end of the long journey. But then we ran out of gas. At first, the 'Captain' thought that he was doing something wrong so he kept trying to restart the motor. That caused the boat to rock in crazy ways. People started crying, some started fighting, others stood up and that caused the boat to tip dangerously to one side and then to the other. Everyone became even more agitated and it seemed that hope was lost. For five hours we were stuck in the middle of the sea with no other boats in sight. People started imagining the worst and several guys wanted to jump off the boat and drown themselves.

At this point, I took out my phone and was surprised that it had a signal and was able to carry a message from me to my brothers. I told them what was happening and said goodbye to them. It would be five hours before I would be able to reach them again to tell them that I had survived the trip.

In some ways, we were lucky; stories I have heard from other people tell of boats that had holes in the side so that when they were in the middle of the strait, the boat started filling with water which they desperately kept bailing out until help could arrive. Other people were not so lucky; their boats failed and sank and they were drowned with just a few hours separating them from their goal of reaching Greek soil. There are cemeteries on the islands that serve as the final resting place for those hundreds of people.

Even though I was also losing hope, I started saying to everybody, "Don't give up hope, there is Greece and there is

Europe. We have been through a lot on our journey and this is the end; just stay calm and pray to God." Everyone started saying the *Shahadat kalema*, which is a Muslim prayer.

A few minutes later a guy shouted and said, "I FOUND THE GREEK COAST GUARD PHONE NUMBER!" There was one problem though, no one could speak English, so I started asking people in Farsi if they knew words in English like "we are" and "sea" and "please help". Then I called the number and asked for help with these English words I had just learned; I couldn't understand their answer. We waited two hours more and finally, the Coast Guard came. Everyone sobbed loudly from happiness and came to me and said you are the only reason we are alive. The Coast Guard took us to the island of Lesvos.

As we were taken onto the Coast Guard boat, we were filled with conflicting emotions. We were happy that we were saved but we didn't know if we would be sent back to Turkey or taken to Greece. We were taken onto the boat but there was no room for our backpacks. So, the Coast Guard officers kept our backpacks on the small boat that had carried us. As we settled into our places on the Coast Guard vessel, we were shocked when we looked back at the rubber dinghy that had brought us to Europe. We couldn't believe our eyes, it looked like a toy, something a child might play with on a beach, not a boat to bring 60 people to safety across a difficult body of water.

Chapter 7
Lesvos

When we arrived at the small harbour, we all had to sit in a line to be searched by Coast Guard officials and then examined by doctors. Firstly though, I jumped from the small boat with a feeling of happiness; we all had arrived in Europe safely, our journey was successful, we felt optimistic about what the future held for us. We kept looking at each other with big smiles on our faces; we couldn't believe how lucky we were. We felt cared for. There was an Afghan woman from our boat in the last month of her pregnancy, and a doctor was there at the dock to make sure that she was OK and to see if she needed any medical care. I joined some of the other guys and started unloading all the backpacks from the other small boat. Each backpack I grabbed filled me with joy; they were signs that we had made it, that we even managed to bring some of our important things with us.

After all the backpacks were unloaded and the first medical check finished, we were lined up and had to undergo a thorough search that included emptying out our backpacks, taking our shoes off, removing our jackets and sweatshirts, enduring a careful pat-down. Nothing could dampen our happiness and relief.

But then with my few words of English, I managed to ask one of the policemen if there was a Wi-Fi signal; I wanted to let my family know that I was safe. To my shock, he kicked me and said roughly, "Why?" Then he continued, mumbling, "Do you want to let the smuggler know you are safe?" This response left me with a fear of the police in Greece that continues to this day, even two years later. The contrast between my happiness and joy and the harshness of the policeman was very difficult to experience. This juxtaposition is one of the big mysteries of Greece to me; the warmth and help of so many people, and the fear inspired by policemen who stop us refugees in the streets and treat us with a complete lack of respect.

The next step after our arrival and search was that we were put onto a bus and transferred to a camp. My biggest concern at that point was to find a Wi-Fi signal so that I could message my family but I still couldn't find one and I was almost hysterical because the last message they had had from me was the goodbye I said to them when I was on the boat. But that thought was soon overwhelmed by other emotions once the bus arrived at Moria. It was like a scene from a horror movie to me. So many people, fences, barbed wire, dusty old tents, dirty clothes hanging up to dry everywhere, crowds roaming with no purpose, people looking emaciated with dull eyes and long hair and expressionless faces, in almost catatonic states, like zombies. The police were treating those crowds roughly, pushing them away from the bus. A group of Afghan residents managed to come up close to us and stared at us and I was completely confused. This is Europe?

This was not my last shock. As we got off the bus, we were registered and given wrist bracelets with our identifying information. We went into a large area and joined a crowd of hundreds of people. We sat there for hours and could see groups of people being led in after us. Food was brought in for us, bread, fruit, macaroni, so we were taken care of. Translators and interpreters were there. The next step for us was to go to a small room for fingerprints and eye scans to verify our identities and nationalities. Since I said I was Afghan, they showed me pictures of Afghani food and asked me to name each dish. They did the same thing with money; they showed me different currencies and asked me to show them Afghani money.

I ended up staying in this reception area for two nights. This was a very uncomfortable place; a large open space surrounded by a high fence. In the middle of the open space, there was a huge tent set up that could fit hundreds of people. There were a number of long benches filled with people waiting for their names to be called. Rumours were flying around the place that we might be in this camp for years, that we couldn't go anywhere, not back to Afghanistan, not forward to somewhere else in Greece or Europe. Everyone was in a state of bewilderment, confusion, and panic, the complete opposite of the joy and happiness everyone felt as they got off the boats. There was constant movement of people leaving this area to go to the main part of the camp and others arriving on the latest buses. Some people were called to the office to be released into the general camp area on their first day here, others on the second or third day. I was lucky. At the end of the second day, they called my name.

At first, they took me to a house loaded with supplies and gave me a towel and other hygiene products. Then because I was an unaccompanied minor, I was sent to a secure place.

I'm sure it was set up like this in order to keep us safe but it felt more like a jail with locks and barbed wire. The police escorted me to this place and I had to pass through a very severe security check. My belt was taken from me, and my shoelaces. There were two sections, section A and section B. I was taken to section B. This ended up being my home for the next 26 days.

But I still had not been able to call my family. In their minds, I had drowned in the sea in the middle of the journey. I kept thinking of this and being completely frustrated that there hadn't been any Wi-Fi in the reception area. I was so worried for them and felt so helpless to relieve their agony. At last, in section B, I had access to Wi-Fi. It wasn't good Wi-Fi, with very weak signals, especially during the day when everyone else was using it. But finally, in the middle of my first night there, I was able to get a good signal and was able to message and call my family. They answered the call with tears of happiness and relief that their prayers had been answered and I was still alive. They had actually been planning a funeral for me when they got the message that brought them the news of my safety.

Once I had spoken with my family, I could relax a little and settle into life in the camp. In the beginning, I was put in a room with a group of Pakistani guys. The rest of the place was organised so that all the Pakistanis were together, all the Pashtuns, all the Hazaras. I felt very lonely and out of place in a room full of Pakistanis. I started talking to the Hazaras about how I could get rid of the Pakistanis and have the Hazaras take over this room, a much bigger and more comfortable room than the room they were staying in. They helped me by coming into my room and hanging out there.

This annoyed the Pakistanis and they finally decided to move to another room with the other Pakistanis. As a result of this, the Hazaras chose me as the leader of our room; I was the one who set the rules: when we would sleep, how we would keep the room clean, when we could use our phones in the room. There was great antipathy though between us and the Pashtuns, who occupied the two rooms on either side of our room.

After I had been there a few weeks, the Pashtuns who lived next to us started harassing us, throwing stones at our door and windows, making loud noises on the roof with Coca Cola bottles filled with rocks, all through the night. We put up with it for the first two nights but finally, on the third night, I told my friends that I was going out to tell them to stop. I went out and started to talk to them but they started making fun of me, "Hazara, you have the courage to tell us anything? You coward" and beating me up. My friends were just standing around, in shock, they didn't want to fight to begin with but they couldn't let me get beaten up. My friends decided to try to stop the fighting but it didn't work until they grabbed me and took me to our room. I was completely bloody. That sight roused everyone else in the room and then they all decided to take action; they went out and started fighting the Pashtuns. By this time, I had recovered enough so I went outside and joined in. In the end, we were maybe 30 people fighting until the police came. They separated us and grabbed us by the arms and hair so that we couldn't move. We had to go back to our rooms and the police stayed there until the morning. I'm somewhat embarrassed now that I look back and see how we were acting; in reality, the situation in Moria was so desperate that people were acting by the law of the jungle; it was only when things became scary that the camp authorities or police stepped in.

At 5 pm the next day, I started a high fever. That's really the last thing I remembered until I woke up in the hospital. I still don't know exactly what happened to me, I never heard the diagnosis. I stayed in the hospital for two days and was given pills to take for the next month. They released me early because I wanted to be in the camp for the celebration of Eid. I went back, celebrated with my friends, and then the next day, my guardian, who had been assigned to me by the NGO *Metadrasi*, came to me and said that I was being sent to Athens.

As I think back again at this time, with the perspective of a few years, it doesn't surprise me that all this fighting went on. And it was not just the fighting between Pashtuns and Hazaras but between all other groups too, even between family members and between friends. The situation we were in was one that caused deep depression and frustration in everyone. Those of us in the unaccompanied section were the fortunate ones; we were living in containers that had bathrooms and running water. We had bunk beds to sleep in and our rooms had electricity. Outside of the area for unaccompanied minors, the situation was desperate. People were crowded into tents that had been put up wherever room was found. They slept on the ground, with no electricity and no water. Bathrooms were beyond filthy so many people chose to relieve themselves in the bushes or on the dirt. There were several faucets throughout the camp for the thousands of people living there. To bathe, a person had to find a bucket and then fill it with whatever water was trickling from the nearest faucet. Food was served three times a day but it took hours and hours to stand in line for each meal. With these conditions, people got sick easily and didn't have access to adequate medical care. The stress and terrible conditions caused anxiety, depression, suicidal thoughts, paranoia, and other psychological trauma.

We had left our countries to flee violence, in search of peace, with hope for our lives, and here we ended up in something that was no better than a concrete jungle, unable to plan our next steps, frightened and discouraged and not knowing what lay ahead.

For me and for the boys in my area, football and volleyball kept us busy for some of the time. In some ways, I felt that I was back in Afghanistan; we played in the evening when it got cooler, and we played in spaces between the buildings in the camp. Our net for volleyball was a rope strung from one building to another and the goalposts for football were two garbage cans. There usually were no balls, so we used whatever was available, plastic bottles, wads of cardboard; the few times there were real balls, they had lost all their air and were just flat wads of plastic. But these games kept us busy and raised our spirits. To our surprise, one day the camp officials took us outside of the camp to a real football field; it was distressing that they took us in vans that had barred windows as if we were prisoners but I was filled with joy. I had never played on a real field; it had been a dream of mine and I couldn't believe that this could happen to me.

There were also other bright spots for me, even in the middle of all this anxiety and suffering. There was an Iranian family I had met on the boat and I ended up in the waiting room with them at the beginning. We talked and talked on that first night and then I fell asleep; in the morning when I woke up, I realised that they had covered me with a light blanket during the night. Another time they came and visited me in the evening while I was in that container with the other unaccompanied minors, I don't think they ever realised how important that visit was to me, how it made me feel like a human being again, in contrast to the chaotic situation around me.

Also, there was a volunteer from Finland, named Nina; she was in Athens while I was in Lesvos but she made a Viber group to encourage me and she helped me in other ways, by sending me a SIM card and by coordinating things with my *Metadrasi* guardian, Niki Krommida. Niki fought hard for my release from Moria. She also treated me like a normal human being again. She took me out of the camp and drove me around the main city of Lesvos and bought me sandals and lunch. I am very grateful for what she did for me; I know that there are many people who have been trapped in Moria for months and months and years but I was able to leave after only 26 days, and I am very grateful for all that she did to make that happen.

Chapter 8
Athens

While I was getting ready to leave, some of the guys in the camp were crying. I had only been there for 26 days and now I was on my way to Athens, while many of them had been there for months and months and had no idea when they would be able to leave. And yet they were all looking towards their unknown future with some hope. We hugged each other and said we'd meet up again in Athens or Germany or Sweden in a few months or next year or in the year after that. That day there were ten of us who left, all unaccompanied minors, all with guardians from *Metadrasi* Big black vans came to pick us up, so we no longer felt like prisoners. These were comfortable vans with regular seats and windows without bars; we almost felt like we were the president of a country to travel in vans like this. The vans dropped us off at the port, the ten of us along with all the *Metadrasi* staff members. We got on the ferry, and I remember how big it was and that it was painted dark blue. We were allowed to walk around the boat until 11 in the evening. We wandered around and played cards and ate dinner, always accompanied by the *Metadrasi* staff. It was a delicious taste of freedom. We were surrounded by Greeks and other Europeans and Americans travelling from Lesvos back to Athens, our first encounter outside of the camp with a way of life we could barely imagine.

Alongside that taste of freedom was some shock as we encountered western culture for the first time on a ferry in the Greek summer. How to make sense of women who didn't wear veils, who walked around in shorts and tank tops, of men and women sitting together and talking together and sometimes even touching each other? How to figure out how to use western toilets? What kind of a boat was this, there were bathrooms with showers, bedrooms, restaurants, it seemed like a city on water and I couldn't figure out where the electricity came from. Here I was, a young boy from Afghanistan, a refugee, who had just made his way from Baghlan to Lesvos but I was most amazed and confounded by a ferry boat in the Aegean.

At 11 pm, we were supposed to go into the cabins to go to bed. But we were so excited by the newness of everything we were seeing, that we had no desire to go to a little room and shut ourselves off from the beautiful night sea, the crowds of people roaming the decks, the lights of the islands in the distance, the sound of the boat engines. The *Metadrasi* staff had to chase us and round us up and take us to our rooms. There were three of us and one staff member from *Metadrasi* in my room. As soon as we settled in, we fell asleep at once, feeling comfortable and safe at night for the first time in a long time. And we felt special since we were sleeping on new, clean sheets in an air-conditioned cabin.

The *Metadrasi* guardian was a young woman and obviously, her role was to keep us safe since that NGO had taken on legal responsibility for us. She stayed with us in our cabin and didn't sleep at all that night and she didn't even

98

speak with us; she felt the weight of her responsibilities and didn't want to let anything get in the way of fulfilling them. I hoped that she was not looking at us as threats but as the vulnerable human beings we were. We were grateful for her and for all the efforts of *Metadrasi* to get us out of the hell that was Moria.

My education of life in the west was beginning now. It hadn't begun in Moria, where there had been no educational programs and no real social programming. Although I had started to learn English on my own in Moria, I was relying on YouTube videos (downloaded late at night when the very weak internet had the strongest signal) and had only begun to master the most basic phrases. I had learned no Greek except for the all-purpose swear word *malaka*. Now I was eager to take it all in and begin my new life.

The boat docked in Piraeus, the port of Athens, as the sun was coming up. The first day of my life in the big city of Athens. We disembarked and found some taxis that were waiting for us. My expectations were low; I was expecting to be delivered to another Moria. But I, along with three other guys, had won the lottery and was brought to the shelter for unaccompanied minors run by the NGO Faros, which had to be one of the best shelters in Athens. There I finally felt like a normal human being again. There were 20 other guys living there, from Afghanistan, Pakistan, Syria, Iraq, Morocco. There was a lot of food, a social worker, and many other staff members to take care of me. I made friends, I was safe, I was free to go all around Athens. We had football, we went to the movies, and we had many other activities. I also went to school and was able to study English.

But one of my first impressions had to do with a face in a window. As we climbed out of the taxi, I looked closely at the building that was to be my new home. Although the building and the street must have been beautiful decades ago, now the street was run down, the pavement full of holes, and many of the buildings lining the street had been abandoned and were in terrible condition; one that had been renovated was a hotel that I later learned was used by prostitutes. The Faros building had been renovated on the inside but from the outside, it still had a harsh and grim look. As I was looking at it closely, I noticed someone looking out at the window on the ground level. He began smiling at us and then waved to us and welcomed us. To have a European smile at me and make me feel at home was an amazing experience. It made me feel comfortable being there and gave me hope that I could find a home in this strange city.

As I look back now, I realise how truly lucky I was. Others spend months and even years in Moria and on the other islands, in inhumane conditions and unable to leave. Some succumb to depression and a lethargy born of living without hope and dignity, others leave illegally and then find themselves in Athens unable to find housing or cash assistance or to apply for the documents that would make it legal for them to work. You can see them even today, aimlessly wandering Viktoria Square and the surrounding streets, trying to find purpose in lives that have been denied the possibility of the most basic human needs.

But for me, life became good. I was able to roam the streets of Athens and learn about the city. I made good friends with the other boys and many of the staff members. My favourite activity was football; we formed a team with the other boys at the shelter and I was ecstatic to see that at least two of my friends were amazing players. I was the goalie, a position I love. We had practice at least once a week, and we set up games with various other teams throughout the city. Because of the three of us who were the heart of the team, we usually had easy victories. When we didn't have games scheduled, we played wherever we could find, even in a small open space. The paved entrance to the National Archaeological Museum was one of our usual spots. The museum was close to our shelter and the space was open and tree-lined; the goalposts on each end were spaces between trees. I cannot begin to describe the joy that those games gave me. They also taught me a street style of play, even today my football teammates at school tease me for the tough and scrappy way I play.

There were other activities that I also liked a lot. We went to an amusement park, we went to the movies, we had foosball and ping-pong tournaments, and I learned to play chess, something that has become a passion of mine. My teacher was Ibrahim, one of the staff members, an Iranian who had lived in Greece for decades with his Greek wife and children. He was a really intense, powerful, and impressive man whom I looked up to. He became not just my chess teacher but a model to me on how to be a strong and good man. At that time, I couldn't even imagine that there would ever be a time that I could beat him in chess. He was wise and thought deeply and strategically and I could only hope to imitate those qualities in my own way. Right now, I am back in Athens for a summer vacation to see my mother. I have spent some time at Faros and I played several games with Ibrahim. I was so happy to see how much better a player I had become from the time that I played my first games with him.

There were things that were difficult for me at Faros. The food was a problem for most of us boys. We had a hard time adapting to Greek food and the kitchen staff had a hard time figuring out how to adapt to the tastes of all of us. The rooms became very crowded as more boys arrived in the shelter, with anywhere from six to ten boys in small rooms, leaving no space to even walk around. Meal hours were fixed and there were times I came home from school and couldn't eat lunch because lunch was over.

The conditions had a feeling of being somewhat chaotic, a situation not only faced by Faros but by almost all of the NGOs in Athens at that time, trying to respond to a situation that changed almost daily, with new arrivals, changing asylum policies and procedures, refugees who were becoming impatient with bureaucratic delays and who were beginning to lose hope.

School was also a problem for me. I had been eager to go back to school and so I was happy to be enrolled in a middle school only a few blocks from my shelter. It was in an old building, just a block away from the National Archaeological Museum. I was put into the seventh grade. I found a mini UN in my school; children from Ukraine, Albania, Bulgaria, Afghanistan, Syria, Iraq, China, Bangladesh, Australia, and of course, Greece. I took classes in science, math, history, religion, art, Greek. Actually, I took about 16 classes and in most of them, I didn't learn a thing. I was put into classes, with no support for learning Greek, except for a class each day to teach the elements of the language, starting with the alphabet. But there was no help for coping with the Greek in my classes. I was only able to pass with the help of some generous teachers who would give me tests in English. I would study a subject the night before a test with the help of staff at Faros, and then because I could understand the subject matter and learn it well, I could pass the tests. By the end of the year, I think I had been successful enough to pass seventh grade but I'm not completely sure because I never was able to get the necessary papers I needed to confirm that.

There was one incident that was very upsetting to me and revealed part of my personality that I hadn't realised before. My religion teacher was not very friendly to me throughout the year. One day he had had enough. It was hard for me to pay attention in class since I didn't understand one word, so I would be distracted all period or looking at my phone. On that day, he started shouting at me, "Get out, get out!" He sent me to the principal's office and I was punished by having to sit in an empty office by myself. I sat there and cried and cried. I finally spoke to the principal and he told me that I did not have to go back to the class for the rest of the year. I believe that the fact that I was Muslim made it difficult for the teacher to tolerate my presence in class.

My tears and my reaction when I got back to Faros, though, were intense. When I got back to Faros, I stormed up the stairs and when I realised that there was no food because the lunch hours were over, I could not control my anger. I banged around the kitchen, yelling and punching the wall. It took a long time to calm down. And since then I have found myself reacting like this in other situations. When I feel my dignity being challenged or find myself being humiliated, I can feel the anger coursing through my body and it always takes time to calm down again. One of the things that can help me the most to calm down is talking to my mother who has the ability to speak with me in a way that helps me get rid of my anger.

The first day I arrived at Faros was filled with surprises for me; there was a kitchen, a dining room, a chef who prepared meals just for us. But the one that made me happiest was when I heard that I could take English classes there. Since the time I had learned those few words of English on the boat, I realised how important it would be for my future to be able to understand and speak English. I looked at language as the key to opening a treasure hidden inside a box. And I couldn't believe my luck that I could begin my study of English right in the place where I lived. In my first interview with the social worker there, I told her how important education was to me and she told me about the classes. The next class was in two days and I told her that I would be there. She informed the teacher and also told the teacher that I was very eager and asked her if she would give me some extra lessons in addition to the class that happened only two times a week. It was wonderful for me when I heard that she would do that. I really felt that I was at the beginning of my new life and my new journey.

But at that time, I didn't realise how much a change that would bring into my life. Yes, I started classes and started meeting with the teacher for an hour after each class. My teacher's name was Kathleen and she was an American who had come to Athens because she loved Greece and because she wanted to work with refugees. She was teaching the boys in our shelter and also working at the women's centre sponsored by Faros. We had a lot of fun when we worked together after class. We started going to nearby cafés for our sessions because of the noise level in the shelter. That made us start getting closer and closer. Within a few months, she had become exactly like a mother to me.

The first time we went to a café was an incredible experience for me. Since arriving in Athens, I had seen people sitting in cafés and I wondered if I would ever have that experience. I doubted I would; I was a refugee, and although I was being taken care of, I had no money and I even had no idea how to enter a café and find a place to sit, let alone order something and pay for it. But now here I was sitting in a café with my teacher. I ordered a tea and she did too. The tea came with a pot of water and the tea bag and the cup and I had no idea what to do, so I just watched my teacher carefully and followed what she did. I couldn't believe what was happening to me, I was sitting in a café with an American woman, and I felt like I was a human being again. I was a boy who not long ago had to beg for just a sip of water and now here I was.

We kept getting closer and closer; we sat in more cafés and had more lessons. She became someone very special to me. She treated me just as if I were her son. When I had a sore throat, we went from pharmacy to pharmacy in search of the kind of lozenges she wanted for me, and then she had to teach me how to suck on the lozenge and let it soothe my throat. In December, she had to go back to the US to change her visa. Before she left, she took me clothes shopping for a winter coat and boots. I could see that she was treating me just as she would her own child. She didn't make me feel like I had nothing and she was giving me something but that I was her son and, of course, since it was almost winter, I needed winter clothes to stay warm. We learned a lot about each other on that shopping trip; she learned what size clothes I wore and that I had definite tastes about what clothes I would wear. She laughed at that and understood and didn't get annoyed.

Then we went for the first time to a restaurant to have dinner together. I had stuffed tomatoes and they tasted just like Persian cooking and I was so happy that I called my brother in Afghanistan to show him the food and the clothes while we were still sitting at the table. This was such an amazing afternoon for me; for the first time in my life, someone was buying clothes just for me and buying exactly the clothes I wanted. I kept repeating over and over that I felt like a human being again.

We stayed in touch while she was away, and when Kathleen returned from the US a few months later, we became inseparable. I would meet her as soon as school ended and we would spend hours and hours reading the first *Harry Potter* book in English. Every day we chose a different café and then would sit there making our way through the book. Even today I feel that that's when I really began to learn English, and it was the first book I had ever read in my life, even in my native Dari. On days that I got out of school early, I would run over to the women's centre where she was teaching English to women and girls. I would poke my head through the window to show her that I was there and she would smile back at me and signal me to come into the centre. Sometimes she used me as a translator when she was teaching a new grammatical concept or phrase and her students were confused.

But the most important thing for me was that I had someone in my life who understood me, who listened to me, who made me feel that I was the world to her. It had been seven years since my mother died, and I was just a little boy then. Here I was a teenager, with traumatic experiences behind me, and finally, I had someone to talk to, someone who could help me understand why I was feeling the way I felt in most situations, someone who could console me, encourage me, cry with me, feel my frustration. I spoke openly to her about everything and knew that I could always count on her. I started calling her "Mom" and she considers me her son. I know that she will be there for me forever.

From almost the first moment that I arrived in Greece; the process had been put in place for me to eventually move to Finland. My brother Alijan had been living there for two years and I could join him under the terms of family reunification. This became a complicated emotional situation for me. I really wanted to go to Finland to be able to live near my brother, to be close to someone from my family, but at the same time, I didn't want to leave my mother. She couldn't become my guardian in Greece because she had not yet received her residence permit. It was a difficult situation; we were as close as any mother and son but we had no legal ties. In the end, we decided to move forward with the family reunification and see what could happen after that.

Finally, after several meetings with the asylum service and with the help of my guardian from *Metadrasi*, the date was set for my move to Finland in early June 2017. My mother made the decision to accompany me and then to stay in Helsinki for a few days to help me settle in. In the meantime, I finished seventh grade in the Greek school, spent a lot of time with my friends from the Faros shelter, and spent hours every day reading *Harry Potter* with my mother. The days and weeks went quickly. I was sad to leave but excited to see my brother after three years. He told me I would probably be sent to Helsinki and that there I would have the possibility of studying in a school that taught in English. And so it was with those mixed feelings that I looked forward to the day of my move.

The night before I left was a very emotional one at Faros. I stayed up all night with all my friends. They were excited for me to be joining my brother and going to Finland but also, they were sad because we had become such close friends. My mother had given me little money so that we could have a party; one of the workers at the shelter went out and bought cookies for us. We stayed up all night, celebrating and playing cards and having a good time, enjoying each other's company. For me, though, it was also one more time on my journey when I had to say goodbye to a place that had been important to me, to friends I had gained, to a life that had been mine for the past nine months. My emotions were very high and I felt super sensitive to everything that was happening to me.

Chapter 9
Finland

All my friends accompanied me out into the street in the early hours of the morning, when Christina, my guardian, picked my mother and me up from Faros to take us to the airport.

We arrived quickly and were met by the asylum police who checked my papers and gave me the documents I needed for my trip. It was the easiest check-in for a flight ever. The asylum police went to the ticket counter and within minutes we and our luggage were checked in. But then the long wait; we needed to be at the airport six hours before our flight in order to be there when the immigration officials were on duty, so we sat in the Aegean Airlines lounge and read and talked and tried to keep our emotions under control. One thing that kept going through my mind was the contrast between the ease of my trip to Finland compared to the trips of the thousands of other refugees who tried to get to other countries illegally. Their experiences ranged from getting through security with fake passports or getting caught, from ripping up their Greek or Iranian or Afghani documents and flushing them down the toilet on planes so they could ask for asylum in the country they arrived at, to try to hide on the underbelly of trucks as they drove onto ferries that were headed to Italy.

In the face of all that suffering and discomfort, my few hours of waiting at the airport were nothing.

When it was finally time to go to the gate, there were several surprises. The first was a good one; we were whisked through security since we were accompanied by two Greek policemen. But the next surprise was a tough one. When it was time for all the passengers to get onto the bus that would take us to the plane, the police called us to the front desk and took my mother and me to the first bus. To our shock, the bus took off with just the two of us on board. I felt so embarrassed; did they think I was some kind of criminal that had to be separated from everybody else? Or that I was like a contagious disease? On the other hand, it was nice to have a bus all to ourselves, much more comfortable and so unlike many of the other bus and pickup and taxi trips I had taken on my long journey.

We boarded the plane first and were given seats in the very last row. We were also told to stay on the plane until the police came to take us off. I was so happy to be on the plane with my mother and to be greeted so politely by the flight attendants, who helped me put my guitar in the overhead bin; I made a direct comparison in my mind with their courtesy and with the way I had been treated by smugglers in my previous travels. This was my first plane trip and that was exciting for me, a big first for a boy from a tiny village in Afghanistan.

Everything was new; the view of the clouds from the window, the friendliness of the other passengers, the lunch that was served. I couldn't figure out how they cooked meals on a plane or how the toilet worked, and I needed help figuring out how to lock the bathroom door and was worried that I wouldn't be able to unlock it.

As the flight continued, I was full of excitement and anticipation the closer we got to Finland.

When we arrived, we were the last ones to leave the plane; we had to wait ten minutes for the police to come. During that time, I was so impatient, I wanted to see my brother and begin my new life. When we finally entered the terminal, I was happy and surprised that the police stood to the side to give me space and time to reunite with my brother. He was standing there with tears of happiness and with the biggest smile on his face. I couldn't wait and just ran up to him. I was crying too and laughing and I took him in my arms and just wanted to be in his arms forever.

From the corner of my eye, I could see some other people there waiting for me. After finally letting go of me, my brother introduced me to his friends, Amir and Amir's father Ali Soltani and to two refugee rights activists, Nina and Joanna. They were so warm and welcoming to me that I felt I had reached a place where I belonged, where my journey could end, where I could begin to build a new life.

After many hugs and short bursts of conversation, the police came up to us and told me to come with them to their office. I was excited to hear what would happen. I was thinking that I would be placed in Helsinki, close to my new friends and that I could finally begin to study seriously in English and learn Finnish and get to know the city of Helsinki.

I was led to an office by the police, and my brother Alijan with his friend Amir were with me to act as translators. My fingerprints were taken and my height measured but otherwise, I had no idea what was going on since everything was in Finnish. There was only one moment when the policeman turned to me and said in English, "Do you like Finland?" It seemed to me a funny question since I had just landed a few minutes earlier but he was waiting for my answer.

The only answer I could think of was, "I wouldn't have come to Finland if I didn't like it." I felt a little threatened by the question but now I realise that he probably was just trying to include me in the conversation by asking the simplest thing he could in English.

And then everything I had been hoping for disappeared. I was told that I was being sent to a camp in Oravainen, a tiny village 500 km away from Helsinki, 60 km away from the nearest town. Far from my brother, far from my new friends, far from the possibility of a school in English, and how could my mother ever come to visit me?

The decision was made that I would take the train the next day with my brother to Oravainen but I would spend the night in a camp in Espoo, a suburb of Helsinki. I completely fell apart as I realised the new reality that was facing me. As we walked out of the police station, I went ahead of Alijan and Amir, I needed to be alone to cope with the strong emotions I was feeling. I was sobbing and I couldn't bear the way things had turned out, so different from what I had been anticipating.

On my way to the terminal again, where everyone was waiting, I saw my friend Irma waiting for me, smiling and holding a box of candy to welcome me to Finland. Irma is a journalist and I had met her in Athens, where she had been researching articles on the refugee situation there, she had heard about me from journalist friends who had done a documentary about my brother Alijan and who had interviewed me in Athens. We met up there when she came to Athens in the summer, my mother and I had tea with her one afternoon and became friends with her. It was so kind of her to be at the airport to greet me. It was a long way from the sunny café in front of the National Museum in Athens to the chilly terminal on a drizzly and cool afternoon in Finland. She greeted me in English but I couldn't understand what she was saying because I was so upset and still crying uncontrollably.

In the terminal again, I was quickly surrounded by Nina and Joanna and Ali Soltani and Alijan and Amir, and everyone was talking to me and trying to understand what was going on but I couldn't understand what they were saying and I continued crying and worrying about what was going to happen to me. Then I saw my mom in the waiting room and went up to her. Nothing could calm me down except taking my mother's hands and talking to her and telling her what had happened. We talked for a few minutes, she calmed me down, and I trusted her when she told me that it would all be OK and to just follow the plans that were being made for that night and the next day.

There was much confusion after that. We all headed out for the camp I had been assigned for the night. It was about half an hour away from the airport. We followed the directions given to us but when we arrived at the house where the camp was supposed to be, everything was locked up and clearly no one had been living there for months. Nina made a few calls and I was told to go to another camp not too far away. Irma took my mom back to her hotel, and Alijan and Amir and Ali Soltani stayed with me in the new camp, playing chess with me, talking with me, trying to keep my spirits up. But finally, they left for the night, and I was alone in a new country, in a strange place deep in the woods, in a building isolated from other buildings. I was upset and exhausted and also haunted by memories of being alone in other forests like the ones in Iran on my journey so many months earlier.

The asylum service arranged with the staff at the camp for me to take a train to Oravainen at 12:30 the next day. When I woke up, I called my mother and asked her to come to see me at the camp. Alijan had arrived already because he was going to go with me to the train station along with a staff member, and then accompany me on the train ride. I started feeling better in the car because the staff member Peter spoke English and was very nice to me. When we reached Helsinki, Peter dropped us off in Kamppi, an area Alijan didn't know very well. We got lost and took a long time to find the station. It was clear that I would miss my train.

In the meantime, my mother never arrived at the camp because of problems with the directions, but she managed to call Alijan and they made plans for us to meet at the train station. She arrived before we did, and she didn't know, of course, that we were going to be late. She thought we were already on the train that was getting ready to leave the station. She was so upset that I might be leaving without having the opportunity to say goodbye. She walked up and down alongside the train, peering into the windows to see if she could see me. She couldn't find me and started crying as she continued looking frantically. As the train started pulling out of the station, she walked back down the tracks, when she saw me standing at the end of the tracks with Alijan and Irma. That was when she realised that I had missed the train. She ran up to me and hugged me tightly and sobbed for several moments.

Missing the train was the best thing that could have happened. We all went across the street and sat at a café and drank tea and coffee and ate doughnuts. The asylum service notified us that they had booked me on the train that would leave at 4:30. When we heard that, my mother made the decision to come with me on the train. She ran to buy her ticket and then went back to her hotel to get the things she would need.

Everything went smoothly with the trip after that. We got on the train and then realised that we all had been assigned seats in different cars. So, my mom and I gathered up our things and moved to a table in the dining car where we sat for the entire five hours of the trip. Alijan kept his seat but came in to see us every few hours. I sat very close to my mom and put my head on her lap. At each station, we counted how many stops until ours and we watched through the windows as the landscape changed from the city to small towns to the forest. Since we were heading north and it was June, it never got dark. The light just changed and became not quite so bright.

Finally, we arrived at our stop, Seinäjoki. There was a guy from the camp there waiting to take me and Alijan in his van. But first, he dropped my mom off at a hotel in a nearby town, Pietarsaari. She was going to sit in the only restaurant in that town that was open and then take a taxi back to the train station to catch her train at 1 am.

My mom got out of the van in front of the hotel. She said goodbye to the guy from the camp and to Alijan. I jumped out and stood in front of her. We could barely say anything. We hugged and looked at each other and said our goodbyes with our eyes. Then I turned and went back into the van and we drove off.

As we pulled away, I wondered how many times I was going to keep saying goodbye to the people I love.

The driver drove for another hour, deep into the forest, to my new home. Alijan stayed with me for a few hours until his host father came to pick him up. Alijan handed me a package from Ali Soltani, a care package of some food to eat until I got used to Finnish food. Alijan's foster father also brought food when he came, bags of candies, chips, and bottles of Coca Cola. The sun was still shining when they left at 11:45 pm.

I locked myself in my room. The next day I came out just to eat, and I didn't want to talk to anybody or get to know the other boys or meet the staff. I stayed like this for several days until on Friday I had a meeting with my social worker and the guardian who had been assigned to me by the Finnish Asylum Service.

They asked me about my story and my life, and they asked why I came to Finland. I tried to talk about my past but it was very hard for me to remember everything and explain, to figure out exactly what they wanted to know. Also, I didn't know how much to trust them, so that made me very careful. I said I came to Finland because my brother is here, that Finland is one of the safest countries in the world, and that it is known for its excellent educational system. I talked about how important my education was to me, that I didn't want to lose any more time, and that I wanted to study seriously so I could go to a university. I was upset by the answer my guardian gave me. She told me to stop talking about education, to stop pressuring them about that. Then she said the thing that shocked me the most: "Yes, Finland does have a very good educational system, for the Finns, not for you."

I was pretty devastated by this, so when they asked me what I wanted, I replied that I just wanted to get out of Oravainen. They wanted to know why I felt like that. I said that I cannot live here in the woods, so isolated, that I am getting depressed, and it is getting worse day by day. I want to get into the eighth grade; I don't want to lose any more time for my education. This conversation took us two hours until it finally ended.

Not only was I completely disappointed by this discussion about school but the idea of living in such an isolated place, with no programs set up to educate us or entertain us, reminded me of all the times in the past when I had been in similar situations, alone, in some remote place, having to rely on my own inner strength to keep from going crazy. And it did turn out that as time passed, it got harder and harder for me to keep my balance. I spent almost all my time being on Facebook, and that made me feel worse, to see all the friends that I missed, to see people taking steps forward in their lives, to see the tragedies in Afghanistan. It became harder and harder for me. I began to eat enormous quantities of chips and cookies and to drink Coca Cola, things I had never done before.

It was also at this time that I learned from Facebook that Hassan, my hero from the pickup trip to Iran, the guy who inspired me with his strength and courage, had died. Even though the last time I saw him in Tehran he was a mess and very involved with drugs, I still held out hope that he would be able to turn things around; he was Hassan, after all, so strong, so brave. But that never happened and it turned out that he was deported by Iran and sent back to Afghanistan. When he got back there, the only job he could find was to join the army. He understood the dangers but he needed the money desperately to feed his family. I never learned the details but he had been in the army just a few months before he was killed in a night-time attack on the base where he was living, along with a large number of other soldiers. Learning this was a huge blow to me, coming on top of my inability to get used to living in such a remote place, with no friends or family around to help me deal with that loss.

I didn't know then, but learned later, that sending young refugees to such remote places is one way that Finland deals with refugees. The central part of the country, very thinly populated, is dotted with camps just like this one. It felt like they were trying to keep us out of sight from the rest of the world. How could I become a part of Finnish society if I never even saw any person other than the kids in my camp? How could they expect good behaviour from kids who are shut off from all the rhythms of normal life? Some of the guys in my camp had been there for two or three years, although they did go to school during the school year. There were occasional swim lessons, and one weekend trip to Oulu, a big city several hours away. I realised, even when the other guys were being mean to me, that they were probably acting that way because of the way they had lived the past years, without any feeling of dignity, with a feeling of being not wanted, with a lot of teenage energy but nowhere to use it in a positive way.

I continued to cut myself off from all the other boys in my house for the next few weeks. I just locked myself inside my room. One day I tried to go out and play billiards but it ended up in a big fight. There were 14 other children in my camp, and they were all Arabs, I was the only one from Afghanistan. I know just a few words of Arabic and they knew no Farsi, so it was very difficult to communicate with them. They started bullying me. I was in a situation of feeling very vulnerable, so if they even just looked at me and laughed, I felt sure that they were laughing at me. Life was getting harder.

So, I spent two months without talking to anyone and locking myself in the room. My mom was the only one I talked to and she was everything to me at that time, even though she was in another country, still she was the closest person to me. After I had been in Oravainen for almost two months, my mother decided to go to Helsinki to find a school for me there. To my surprise, the camp allowed me to join her there. This was one of the first signs of hope for me. I started to feel that I could maybe begin my life again; a good school, a big city, things to do, girls to see, friends to make.

When my mother had come to Finland with me in June, she had four days in Helsinki after she returned from Oravainen. She had used that time to meet with refugee activists and learn everything she could about the refugee situation in Finland. The most important piece of information she learned was that if I could be accepted at a school in Helsinki, Migri (Finnish Immigration) was obligated to find me a place to live there. And so she spent the next two months researching schools in Helsinki and finding ones that had programs that would be good for me. She wrote letters to six schools explaining my situation and asking if they would consider me for admission. She received very nice letters in return but for most schools, I would need to take a test in Finnish. The head of one school, the International School of Helsinki, wrote that he would like to meet with us. So, at the end of July, I headed to Helsinki from Oravainen and my mom from Athens, and we prepared for our meeting with Peter

Welch, the ISH head. She had been hoping that one person would read her letter with his heart, and Mr Welch did just that.

It was hard at first for me to come to Helsinki and go for an interview; I had lost all my confidence in the past two months. But I was so excited to go to a city, to see my mother, and to see this school, a completely different experience and feelings from my first day in Helsinki. I was so happy, imagining the time I would spend with my mother, walking through the city, sitting in cafés, spending hours talking, listening to her laugh, watching her smile. She would be very loud and move her arms in cafés when she was explaining something to me; she loves to teach and she does it with energy. It made me smile to myself because I couldn't wait to see her. Even today I'd love to go back to the day I met her then; it made me feel alive again after two months of depression and loneliness.

I was accompanied on the train ride by a staff member, who needed to see my mother and give her approval for me to stay with my mother in Helsinki. Even the train ride was fun because the staff member and I both fell asleep at different times and filmed each other as we were snoring and sent the videos back to the camp. It made the journey go quickly. My mother was there when the train pulled into the station. It was so good to see her standing there smiling. I got off the train and we hugged for a long time and then she had a good conversation with the staff member and everything went smoothly. We left for our hotel to go and have dinner and get ready for the interview the next day at ISH.

As we started talking about what the interview would be like, I panicked and told my mother that I didn't want to go to the meeting. I felt that way because my recent interactions with people in positions of authority had been so difficult and had left me feeling very vulnerable. I was expecting an experience like the interviews with the asylum police and workers or like the questions that people ask you as soon as they learn that you are a refugee. I was feeling very sensitive as a result of the difficult weeks in Oravainen and I didn't want to have to go through that kind of experience. I didn't think I could stand it if the headmaster looked down at me and judged me harshly and refused to accept me. My mom said, "No! You have to go to this meeting." Then I said nothing but turned my back and fell asleep.

The next morning, we woke up and got ready and walked the mile to the school. The head of the school was standing in front of the entrance door. He guided us to his office. I was feeling nervous, anxious, lost, and intimidated, understanding that my future depended on the results of this meeting. I had never before had a meeting with the head of a school and I also felt a lot of pressure because I had to speak English and I was hoping he wouldn't judge my language. It was still less than a year that I had been learning English, so I felt very self-conscious. I shouldn't have, because Mr Welch was a master at talking to students. He was able to make one statement that opened up a whole world. I found myself very comfortable, telling him about my life in Afghanistan, my journey, my life in Greece, my life in Finland, and all my hopes and dreams. He gave us a tour of the school, which was unlike any other school I had seen, with a gym and a lunchroom, many bright classrooms, computers everywhere.

Almost no one else was in the school that day. It was the end of summer vacation but you could tell from the bright colours and the warm atmosphere and the school motto written in large letters that it was a good place for children. Mr Welch pointed out to me the motto of the school, "We empower our students and inspire one another to take thoughtful action." He asked me if I understood. And then I saw the symbol of the school, the snowflake, which illustrates the idea that each student is unique. I was amazed that a school like this existed but I was feeling more and more that it would be an impossible dream to go there. At the end of our tour, we went back to his office and he turned to me and said, "Our door is open for you." It was one of the happiest times in my life when I heard those words. I just sat there in disbelief and excitement as my mom and Mr Welch discussed details of what the next step would be. She had been looking for someone to read her letter with his heart, and here he was, and now they were figuring out what needed to be done for me to be a student there.

My mother and I celebrated our happiness by dancing down the street and walking all through the city with big smiles on our faces. We walked through the farmers' market on the harbour, and we ate ice cream looking out at the water, and walked past other important buildings including the university, beginning to be able to see a future for me like the one I had dreamed of. We had a few more days in Helsinki having fun, sitting in our favourite cafés drinking coffee and tea, and visiting friends at their beautiful houses in the suburbs. The days passed quickly and then I needed to go back to Oravainen and she needed to return to Athens.

We walked to the train station together and she took the bus to go to the airport and I took the train to go back to Oravainen. On the train, I was thinking that everyone in the camp would be happy that such an amazing thing had happened and that I had the opportunity to be a student at such a prestigious school. I was shocked when I arrived to find that no one cared. In fact, in the camp, most of the staff were upset that we had taken the steps on our own to get me into ISH. It made me wonder if they felt that way because they thought that should not be a possibility for a refugee, that no refugee deserved such an education. And it wasn't just that they were upset, they actually started to make it clear that they had no intention of doing anything to help me get out of Oravainen, although they knew how unhappy I was there. Moving to Helsinki was in their hands, since I needed the approval of the social worker and the manager of the camp and they needed to coordinate with Migri, but they didn't do anything at all for a few weeks, and even said bad things about my mother, blaming her for putting such ideas into my head.

In those few weeks, I became more and more upset and depressed and even came close to trying to kill myself one night. Facebook was full of stories of other Afghan boys in Europe who killed themselves in desperation because they were being held in isolation and deprived of any kind of life that made them feel like human beings. To me, my situation was just another situation like that.

But there were other times when I said to myself that I just needed to get out of bed and fight for my fate. Because of this I had many conversations with the staff of the house and with my guardian and they all continued to say almost every day that it was impossible to get to Helsinki and into the new school. One day, I had a meeting with my guardian and I was writing down everything she was saying. She got upset at me and asked me why I was writing. "Are you writing this to complain about me to your mom or to someone else that you know?"

Her words were very hard for me to understand and so I just put my notebook down and said, "What do you mean?" I told her that if my writing made her upset, I would stop writing but that I just wanted to write everything down so someday I could look back and see the details of this situation.

More than two weeks passed like this. I argued every day and they keep resisting. During this time, my brother Alijan came to visit me. He was living with a Finnish family in Kurikka, a little town about a 100 km away. His experience had been very different from mine. I think he had had some difficulties when he first came to Finland two years earlier adjusting to life in a camp but then he met his foster family and he felt at home almost immediately. He was an integral part of the family and he studied in the local school and was very active in judo. He never told me about the problems he had had when he first arrived. When he came to see me, he encouraged me and kept telling me to always do my very best work. I never heard him complain and he tried to motivate me when he visited me. I wondered about his struggles and really wanted to know what his experiences had been but he never spoke to me about them, but just kept trying to be an inspiration for me.

Also, during this time, communication with the International School of Helsinki continued. My mother kept them informed of what was happening in Oravainen. Their response was just to keep emphasising that they were waiting for me. They understood that there might be a delay until I could get to Helsinki, and they promised to work with me whenever I arrived and make my transition as smooth as it could be.

In the meantime, the Finnish schools started the new year and I finally got to go to school again, at the local public school 40 km away. I was relieved; I love school and was happy to be back studying again. But on the other hand, I was very upset that I was still in Oravainen because I was so eager to be at ISH. Also, I had been put back into the seventh grade, so I was frustrated that I couldn't move ahead, and I was frustrated that I spent most of my time learning Finnish and had only a few classes in ordinary subjects like math and PE. That meant that I was in special classes just for refugees, and wouldn't have the chance to meet Finnish students and feel like a normal student. Nevertheless, I worked hard. The walls of my room were covered with cards with Finnish vocabulary. And I did get to know some of the Finnish kids and play football with them during recess.

It came as a huge surprise when one Friday afternoon, my mother received an email from the manager of my camp. She told her that my transfer had been approved and that I would be moving to a shelter in Helsinki on the following Wednesday. They told her that they would not tell me until Tuesday evening but she told me right away since she felt that I should have a little warning and time to prepare myself for such a change. That gave me the time to say goodbye to students and teachers at my school and I was really happy to see the reactions of some of my teachers, who told me how much they would miss me, that they wished I could stay there with them. I even spoke with the principal of the school and thanked her for providing an education for refugees, she stood up and shook my hand and wished me good luck. She must have reported my conversation with the manager of my camp because when I got home, the manager came to me and asked if I was sure that I wanted to leave, that the reports about my behaviour and performance at school were so positive that maybe I had changed my mind.

The next few days were filled with excitement. I got my things ready and said goodbye to the staff at my camp. It was somewhat of a relief to me to be able to speak to them with kindness and calm instead of my usual anguish and disappointment and anger, I'm glad we had this chance to repair our relationships. But the truth was that I was so happy to be leaving, couldn't wait to go to my new school, and felt I was finally finding my place in the world.

On my last day in Oravainen, two workers from RUTH'S (the name of my camp there) drove me to the train station and we talked a lot along the way about my new school. In some way, all my worries came out. I said I would be going to a school where most of the children come from wealthy families but that I am a refugee without the kind of money they have, that I don't have the same kind of life they have. Will I have anything in common with them? I was sure I would find a lot of friends there but what would I do if someone invited me to a party? How could I answer them? I wouldn't have the money to join them and couldn't stay out late because of the rules of the camp.

Then one of the workers replied to me, "Jawid, don't worry about these kinds of things. Just focus on your education. We know you are a smart guy; we believe in you, we know you can deal with these kinds of things, we've seen how you fight for what you want." We continued talking like this until we arrived at the train station. We had to wait for the train for about ten minutes. In these moments, we had time for just a few words; I will not forget you, thank you for helping me, don't forget me. When the train came, the staff member Katarina helped me with my two suitcases, my bicycle, my backpack, and my guitar. I settled into my seat and was really happy to make a new friend who was sitting in the seat next to me, a young woman, who also was on her way to Helsinki. We talked a lot until we arrived in Helsinki. We exchanged our numbers, we shared our Facebook, and we are still good friends. She was one of the first Finnish friends not connected to refugees I made and she made me feel much more comfortable and made me understand how friendly and helpful Finnish people are.

Chapter 10

Helsinki

At the Helsinki train station, my friend Irma was there waiting for me together with one of the staff members of my new camp. The staff member took my luggage and gave Irma directions to the camp. Irma handed me a flower as a welcome gift. "You have been through a lot," she said. "And I hope you have a good new life here in Helsinki at your new school."

But the words that touched me the most were, "You are not alone on this journey."

Irma took me to the camp and introduced me to the staff there. Before she left, she gave me a very meaningful gift, a map of the territories conquered by Genghis Khan. Many people consider Genghis Khan and his Mongols as the ancestors of today's Hazara, something I had no idea about at that time. I was grateful to learn something about my history, especially at a time when I was on the verge of a completely new life.

My first few days at the camp were a combination of feelings; nervousness about getting to know the other kids in the camp, most of them were Syrian with just a few Afghans, and excitement because I was back in a city and starting the school of my dreams.

Mostly I was very happy and I felt strongly that I could finally find the childhood that had been so drastically cut off when I left Afghanistan. But I also discovered that sometimes thoughts about my past made me feel sad. My story will always be with me, that is part of life. Sometimes I want to forget it but I can't. But most often, I want to remember it and be proud of what I endured and take strength from that.

"Out of suffering have emerged the strongest souls; the most massive characters are seared with scars." I have always been moved by these words of Khalil Gibran.

The camp itself was very comfortable; it had once been a nursing home. Each one of us had our own room with a bathroom connected to it. There was a big kitchen with refrigerators filled with food. There was a large dining room and a living room with a big-screen TV and lots of games and puzzles. The staff members were young and very caring. The home was located in Espoo, so it took just 30 minutes to get to the centre of Helsinki. Closer to us was a shopping centre with many stores, a public school, and one of the most amazing libraries I have ever seen.

One great thing about the camp was the fact that I had my own room there. Since I was finally feeling settled, I wanted to decorate my room and make it beautiful. I wanted to buy some flowers to put on the table or some other kinds of things to decorate my room, but how could I buy anything since I did not have any money? I finally had the idea to start making some handicrafts from coloured paper that they let me have from the office supplies.

I spent a lot of time making these crafts, learning from the internet. This helped me feel more at home and calmed my nerves before I started my new school.

After I had been in the camp for about a week, I had a message that I had a meeting at the International School of Helsinki. I was invited to visit the school to meet students, look around the school, visit classes, and meet some teachers. I was very excited. There was a staff member from the home where I was living who came with me to visit the school. On the day of the visit, we were running late and I didn't want to be seen by the school as someone who was unpunctual. I was very worried and thought of ways that I could get a message to the school to let them know that I might be late. There were many times that I was saying to the staff member: "Why is it like this? How can I be late on the first visit?" I felt stressed and anxious because I wanted to be on time and make a good impression. In that moment, I didn't want to hear any of the things she was saying to calm me.

In the end, we did arrive on time. I was not late. As I walked through the main entrance, I felt that I was the luckiest and richest person in the world. I felt proud to be in such a privileged school. We went to the office to speak with the Head of the School, Mr Welch, one of the kindest people I have known. He has a good heart, he is able to understand me, and he opened the doors to an education that I thirst for. We had five minutes of chatting but the moment I heard him say, "You will start your studies next week," I felt as though a great gift had been given to me; the gift of humanity, respect, hope. I felt like a famous celebrity at that moment. He took me around the school, introducing me to my classmates and showing me the new classes where I would be learning. After this introduction and some chatting, I went back to the place where I was living, but going from here to there was a different feeling from the way I felt earlier in the morning. I was laughing inside, very happy and thinking about the next step that I would take on this journey. There were other thoughts and questions: "How would I adapt? How would I manage to be in a class with students who speak English? How would I understand the work in English?"

I wanted to prepare myself so that at least I could read something. I had a very short period of time, just three days before I would go to this school for the first time. I went directly to the nearest public library and started to look for books to read to prepare myself. I took two comic books because the other books were very difficult for me because the only book, I had ever read in English was the first *Harry Potter* book that my mom read to me. She explained everything to me then but now all I had were those two comic books. During the three days that I had before I started school, I read those books two or three times, using Google Translate. I did very little else except reading, sometimes even forgetting to eat.

Time passed, the three days of preparation sped by and then, finally, the moment arrived for me to begin my education at ISH, as a student in the eighth grade.

On the first day that I arrived for classes at my new school, I entered through the front doors of the school but this time, I was by myself. I wondered how had the other students arrived on their first day at the school; had they arrived with their families or also alone, like me? Almost immediately I saw Mr Welch, and he smiled at me. It made me feel like he was hoping for the best for me. Mr Thrash was also there, greeting me warmly. At that moment, seeing that both the Headmaster and the Deputy Headmaster were waiting for me made me feel famous. Then I saw one of my classmates who introduced himself as one of the smartest guys. He welcomed me warmly and wanted to take me to the class but before that, I had to meet my advisory teacher, who had the responsibility to give me all the equipment that I needed. The equipment included a class schedule and a MacBook Air. My first challenge (since I had never used a computer before), how to use a MacBook? I didn't even know how to turn it on!

When I look back now at my first few weeks at ISH, I am amazed and shocked at how easily I made the transition there, considering that I was beginning in mid-September while the rest of the students had begun in early August, my English was still at a rather basic level, and I had never written even one paragraph in English. I had no idea what the teachers meant when they spoke about essays, projects, presentations. I couldn't even understand the directions that they gave us in the classroom; I just followed the other kids and did what they did. I was hesitant to ask any student what the homework was because I didn't want them to think I was any less than them. I was, in the beginning, very conscious that I was a refugee and they were the children of bankers and diplomats and professors. Also, I was perhaps too proud to keep asking the teachers to explain every little thing, not wanting to reveal exactly how inexperienced I was with a school like this.

A distinctive feature of ISH is that it follows the International Baccalaureate Program, even in middle school. This program is a very student-centred way of education that is focused on teaching critical thinking skills, research skills, presentation skills, group work. Even for European and American students who come to ISH for the first time, there is a period of transition to a program that is so rigorous. For me, after spending most of my education in an Afghani school and one year in a Greek school where the teaching was done in a much more rigid and traditional way, I felt like I had landed on a different planet. Now, one year later, I am finally mastering this new type of learning, and I am very grateful for everything I have learned. I am confident that my work at ISH will be the best possible preparation I could have for whatever the future holds for me.

One decision I made at the very beginning was not to reveal my identity as a refugee to the other students. The administration of the school and all the teachers knew. Obviously, I would have needs different from other students, at least in the beginning, and the adults in the school needed to know my history so they could help me in the most appropriate way. But I didn't want the students to know. I was worried that they would judge me and not want to be friends with me. My plan was to become friends with them on an equal basis, and then sometime in the future let them know my story.

One thing that was true from the beginning was that I always showed that I was proud to be from Afghanistan. Whenever we could choose a country to research for a project, my hand would shoot up first so that I could choose Afghanistan. It became a joke; as soon as a topic would be assigned, all the kids turned to me and said, "Jawid, Afghanistan, right?"

The most interesting part was that they all thought that I was a very rich kid, with a crazy mother who lived in Athens and who let me live alone in Helsinki. I told them I lived alone and they pictured me in my own apartment, not in the home where I lived with 20 other refugees. They envied me my freedom, not knowing the kinds of rules I had to follow in my camp (being on time for meals, evening curfew, bed checks) or the kinds of things I had to worry about as far as my status in Finland.

My plan worked better than I could have imagined. ISH is a small school with under 500 students. There were only 25 students in the entire eighth grade and I soon became friends with all of them. I was invited to birthday parties, became a part of many clubs, and played football for both the middle and upper school teams. I learned to ice skate, learned what ultimate frisbee was, went on school trips to various museums throughout the city, hung out with my friends after school at Burger King. I was living the life of a normal teenager, something I could hardly have imagined when I was on my journey.

At the same time, I was becoming a part of the Afghan community in Helsinki, a community of about 13,000 Afghans in Finland with the majority living in Helsinki. There are several mosques and a vibrant sense of solidarity. My brother Alijan was very active in the mosque, even though he lived about 500 km away. He had lived in Helsinki when he first arrived in Finland three years earlier. There were many times when I would walk into a room at the mosque or go onto a football field and people would ask me, "Are you Alijan's brother?" I didn't think we looked so similar but other people could spot me right away. I was so happy to be identified as his brother; he was a role model for me in his kindness, his gentleness, his devotion to the community, his sense of responsibility. I also became a part of a group of Afghans who organised a series of conferences throughout the year; the core of this organisation was a group of four of us, all under the age of 18. The conferences were for young people and we always had Afghan speakers who had become successful in Finland who could inspire the younger Afghans and point out paths for them to follow to be able to integrate into Finnish society and build prosperous lives for themselves. I am very grateful for my connections to the mosque and to this organisation, I now have many friends in the Afghan community and feel that I am an integral part of it.

There have been other times, though, when my situation was more difficult for me to handle. My eighth-grade humanities class focused on studying the refugee situation for several months. It was very difficult to be in a classroom where everyone was talking about their ideas about refugees and not to reveal who I really was. And the news was always filled with stories about how it was becoming more common that refugees were not welcomed in Europe. Things were not quiet in Afghanistan; this year was one of the worst as far as attacks throughout the country, and most of the attacks were made against my people, the Hazara.

I also was waiting for the decision of Migri, the immigration service, about my application for a residence permit. Although I had been allowed to come to Finland to be reunited with my brother, I still had to go through the process of applying to get a permit to allow me to stay in Finland. That is always a nerve-wracking and emotional experience. I spent one day at Migri when I made my application, and for almost eight hours they questioned me and made me go through all the reasons I had left my country. They had the power to decide that my reasons were not strong enough and I was worried about that for the months it took until my residence permit was finally approved. Once I received it, I could finally breathe easily. It was well known that at least once a month a plane full of Afghans who were being deported back to Afghanistan took off from the Helsinki airport. My residence permit for four years means that I will be able to finish my high-school education before I have to apply again.

I usually was able to stay emotionally balanced. One thing that helped me immensely was that I knew I had the support of all the adults in the school. I could go to Mr Welch if I needed to. But the person I relied on most of all was the counsellor/psychologist Ms Clarke, whom I was required to meet with once a week. My time with her was the only time during the school day when I could be completely open about what I was feeling. One day everyone from the class went on a field trip but I had to stay at my home for three meetings: with the manager of the house, with the social worker, and with my guardian. Because I had received my residence permit, I had to move to a new home and this meeting was to discuss that. I felt a little vulnerable; I was comfortable with my current home and the idea of having to move made me a little nervous. But the hardest part for me was that I had to miss school for those meetings. So, while all the other students went on a field trip, I had to stay and deal with my life all by myself. The meetings ended at 11:30 and then I rushed to school.

As soon as I arrived, I went straight to Ms Clarke before I went anywhere else. I got very emotional while I was talking to her and suddenly, I started crying and crying. I had always promised to myself that I would never cry but here I was in her office sobbing for 30 minutes. I had always told myself that I was a strong person and now I was feeling that I was not as strong as I thought. Ms Clarke was so kind to me and told me that I needed to cry and shouldn't feel ashamed. After that,

I had science class and the activity that period was to write up a water experiment we had finished. I couldn't figure out what I needed to do because I was still quite emotional. My teacher was very patient and explained the assignment to me many times but I still did not get it and it made me hate myself.

Another day I was in humanities class and we were doing a Model United Nations (MUN) project. One of the first things we had to do, in preparation for the actual MUN conference, was to discuss the topic of the situation of refugees in Europe and to come up with solutions to the challenges that refugees face in Europe. There were many issues that we had to discuss, and one of them was the perception of many Europeans that "refugees are more vulnerable to being recruited into extremist groups, which could pose a threat to the safety of the citizens within a country". My part of the assignment was to come up with a resolution for this. Imagine for a moment, I could use this opportunity to really let them know what I thought of this statement but my mouth was locked, not only because I couldn't find the words to debate but because I felt so frustrated. Their understanding of what it is to be a refugee is summarised in these words: useless, not as smart as Europeans, terrorists, dirty, ignorant. This is not me; I am not any of these things. I have a family and we were happy together, we ate and laughed, we had a home, we worked and had a full life, and I was surrounded by people who loved me.

And so it was very hard for me to hear this discussion about refugees since I was a refugee. They knew me as their friend, as their teammate, as their classmate, and they knew that I was not a terrorist or any other of those things. And yet I was not ready to tell them that I was a refugee and so even though I had so much to say about being a refugee, I couldn't speak. I am a very active student in all my classes but now I felt like my mouth had been chained shut. Because I was feeling pretty vulnerable at this moment, I didn't want to reveal anything that would make them feel sorry for me.

The day was arriving for our actual MUN conference. But before that, I needed to go to my teacher to tell her, "I heard that some of the guys are going to talk against my proposal and they will use the kind of words that will be hard for me to hear, so would it be possible for me to make my speech and leave the class."

My humanities teacher Ms Mikuska was amazing; she always could understand me and she didn't disappoint me now. She spoke, "That's exactly what I was going to recommend to you."

On the day of the conference, I showed up to class with my suit on, ready to take on the role of a diplomat trying to solve one of the big challenges facing Europe. I felt super prepared. I had studied the material hard, had prepared my speech thoroughly, and was confident that my own background would allow me to have a deep perspective that could be very helpful in the task we had in front of us of coming up with a resolution containing our ideas of how Europe should successfully manage the challenge of the millions of refugees who had recently arrived. I wished that I could stay for the whole debate but I felt too fragile, in case the conversation turned to difficult ideas expressing a viewpoint that was against refugees.

Later I heard from other students that my fears had been real. During the debate, one student had said, "Refugees do not deserve to be here in our country and we shouldn't build a wall because it would take money to build it and we shouldn't waste our money on that. Instead, we should make a wall of bullets." The meaning was clear, he was proposing shooting refugees.

My classmates didn't completely understand why I had left the room. When the class was over, they ran up to me to tell me how the discussion had gone. When I heard the words of that student, a curtain of darkness covered my eyes; I just picked up my backpack and walked away. I tried to cover my feelings and started talking to a student from another grade. Leaving at that moment saved me from feelings of anger and frustration at the ignorance that people have about refugees. The irony is that the guy who made this statement about a wall of bullets had been a member of the Model United Nations club for many years and was the chair of the group this year. I was frustrated; his views were compromising his position and it seemed that he hadn't learned anything about the spirit of the UN and the Universal Declaration of Human Rights.

I spoke to Ms Mikuska and told her that it was good I had not been in the class. This was the reason I had to leave, I didn't want to be the same as him and use harsh words that would hurt him.

After this episode, I started isolating myself. I was upset by the violent ideas of that one guy but even more upset that my classmates and friends were laughing at what he had said, treating it as a joke. I started eating alone rather than with other students, didn't go outside at recess to be with the other students, and stopped going to Burger King and McDonald's after school. For the first time since I arrived at ISH, I didn't want to go to school. But I said to myself, "No...you have the responsibility to show them that we refugees are not the way they think. I am not a victim. I can build my future by going to school." And so I kept going to school every day. I didn't miss any classes, even though it was really hard; it was only the support of my teachers that kept me going.

One week later, Ms Mikuska addressed the whole class. That was the day that we combined the two classes together, science and humanities. Ms Mikuska decided to talk about what had happened the day of the conference. She did not invite the guy who spoke of the wall of bullets because she didn't trust how he would behave and because he was in the 11th grade and these were eighth-grade students.

Class started with Ms Mikuska talking about what had happened. She was very emotional; her voice was trembling when she spoke about that class because it was so hard for her also. Ms Bowen, the science teacher, added her comments. It was hard for her to speak because she was trying to keep herself from crying, and because she was upset at the irony of speaking to a Model United Nations group about discrimination. Mr Welch was there too. He talked about the kind of narrow-mindedness that can be harmful for people. At that moment, I felt very emotional but supported. I stayed in the room and I raised my hand and said that I would like to tell how I felt about it. I didn't mention that I was a refugee because I didn't want the other students to know about me yet but I just said, "When I heard the idea that we should not build walls but walls of bullets, it felt like a curtain of darkness surrounded me. It hurt me when my classmates laughed at that statement because I am from Afghanistan and because I represent Afghanistan and all the refugees from my country."

After that, we started working again and the class continued but something changed in me. Speaking out loud was a release for me and I stopped isolating myself. Something shifted; I had been keeping everything inside. I felt like I couldn't say how I felt to other students before because I was afraid they would laugh at me but there in the MUN meeting with the headmaster and the two teachers, the moment was right for a release.

Chapter 11
Ted Talk

This made me start thinking that it was time for me to tell the truth about my story to my classmates. My mother and Mr Welch agreed and encouraged me to find a way to do that. I had a long conversation with Mr Welch who had become such a support for me. His door was always open to me and I felt like I could tell him anything and then trust his response. He helped me to see everything more clearly. He told me about the TEDx conference that ISH would be holding in a few months and he urged me to take that opportunity to tell the story of my journey to the school. It would give me the opportunity to say a lot of things about myself and my life. I was excited. I realised that it was important to let all the students know who I really was. I was tired of having to hide my true story from students who had become my friends. But I was also nervous. Will there be people who will stop being my friends when they learn that I am a refugee? Will they be shocked and then feel sorry for me? Will they joke about it? Will they look at me and see me as less than them? Will they see me as a potential terrorist? I began to realise that doing a TED talk was the best way to reveal my truth; I could control how everyone heard about it, rather than telling small groups at a time and having rumours spread that I couldn't control.

TEDx was going to be the opportunity to speak to the whole school; students, teachers, parents. My chance to speak when everyone is listening, a formal and official moment when the audience is quiet and only I speak. I decided it would be a statement of survival, hope, strength, heroism, and dreams. It would be the story of a brave traveller who left home because it was the mouth of a shark, a young boy who ran for the border when the whole city was running too...running for their lives, running for freedom, running towards the unknown. When I started running, I didn't know that I would end up in an international school with the opportunity for an education but when we run, we leave behind the hopes and dreams we had for our life at home and hope simply to stay alive.

I started having weekly meetings with Mr Welch. In the beginning, we talked in more general terms about what I should include and how to present it. I would write a section every week and then review it with him. Then we started working on the structure of my talk and the photos that would accompany it. These meetings were one of the highlights of my first year at ISH. I felt honoured that the head of the school was giving me an hour of his time every week and I realised as time went on that he really understood me and respected me. It is thanks to him that my TED talk became such a powerful presentation. I will always be so thankful to him.

As the time for the ISH TEDx neared, I struggled to find a title, until I came upon a poem by the British Somali poet Warsan Shire, a poem which is a powerful statement about being a refugee.

I chose the image of the first two lines as the title of my talk, 'The Mouth of a Shark'. I didn't want my friends to know

143

what I was talking about, and this title didn't give it away. "Are you talking about something in biology?" one of my friends asked me. "Come on, tell me. I'm your best friend." It was hard for me to keep my secret for the last few weeks but I was hoping to make my presentation a surprise and I didn't want to ruin it.

I practised and practised my talk in Mr Welch's office, standing in front of the mirror in my room, on the bus. It was always on my mind and I was becoming very excited. It became harder and harder to keep my secret. I had been at ISH for seven months and now I wanted to tell my story.

One of my classmates, Taimi, was also preparing for her TED talk. I was already pretty close to her since she was in all my classes and we often ended up working on projects in the same group. She was intrigued by the title of my talk and so one day she asked me to explain what it meant. I was torn about what I should do. I really wanted to tell her and I was almost sure I could trust her. But I was worried because so many of my classmates had asked me and I hadn't told them. They might get mad at me and the girls might become jealous of Taimi because I had trusted her and not them. But I felt such a strong impulse to tell her. What a relief it would be, to share my thoughts about my story and about the preparation for our talks. I could stop carrying everything inside me and she promised me that she would not tell anyone. So, I made the decision and for the first time, I told the story of my journey to one of my classmates.

With just a week to go before the talk, I am expecting that when people hear my story, they will respond with maturity, curiosity, and admiration. I expect they will have a lot of questions. I also expect that the negative side of humanity could also surface; it could be that someone would say something that revealed a kind of ignorance like the guy who announced at the MUN that refugees should be managed with a wall of bullets. If I do get reactions like that, this would separate for me the people I can trust from the people I cannot trust. It would reveal my true friends from shallow friendships.

I decided that I wanted to have a plan for how I would deal with negative reactions. One response could be to just ignore them. But this would be difficult for me because I am a refugee. I realise that a person who has not walked in my shoes or lived in my country would have a hard time understanding what that has meant for me. My hope was to be able to change the minds of the people listening to me so that they would be able to really comprehend the meaning of my experiences.

The day of the TED talk finally arrived. I was very nervous. I did not sleep the night before; I could not close my eyes for one second. My mind was filled with the things that I would say and how to say them. During that night, I was reliving my journey. As I was practising my speech, I could see in front of my eyes the events that took place almost two years earlier. Although in my normal life now at ISH, I usually tried to keep the memory of everything that happened to me in the back of my mind, I now had to go through it all again to tell my story. There are no words to express what that was like. The thing that motivated me and kept me going through the night was my goal to deliver a clear message and tell people that a refugee is not defined by the words that most of society believes; terrorist, victim, dirty, desperate, needy, a burden on society, impoverished.

On the day of the TEDx event, my senses were blurred. It was as though the world was happening around me in slow motion. I was in class and I could not understand anything that was going on around me. I asked my teachers many times to clarify a point but even when I was trying to ask my questions, I couldn't find the words to speak in English. It was a shock to feel this way and very hard to describe. The teachers asked what was wrong with me, and I explained that I didn't get enough sleep but the feeling still left me confused and very nervous as I thought to myself, *If I can't speak now, how can I do my TED talk?*

That was the moment when I decided that I had to go to Ms Clarke, who was the right person to talk to about this because she could listen and understand me deeply. I just went to her and told her how I was feeling. Then she told me that she knew how this fear of speaking feels. She said that she used to work with people who had to speak to audiences of a thousand and that studies show that the fear of speaking for most people is right up there with the fear of death! But my fear was even harder than that because I wanted to share something so very personal.

I had my weekly counselling session scheduled for that day but I decided to go earlier because I couldn't continue to get through the day. My eyes were closing, my speech was shutting down, my legs could not move, and I had the feeling that my heart would stop beating. I needed sleep.

Ms Clarke did something unusual. She moved the furniture around the room to make a bed and played a guided relaxation. My mind was still very active; all the same thoughts that had kept me awake the night before were still coming to me. I don't know how it happened but my exhaustion overwhelmed me and I fell asleep for an hour and 45 minutes.

By the time I woke up, I saw her kindness. She had put a sign on the door, 'Please do not enter', and she had asked the student who was working on the computer outside the door to stop anyone who tried to knock on the door. She left the room while I was sleeping but when she came back, I was awake and refreshed and practising my TED talk again.

That made me feel that I always have someone who is looking over me and it also encouraged me to be strong. Her trust in me gave me the courage to go out to the auditorium and do my TED talk.

One hour later, I had to give my speech. Before going on stage, I was shaking, thirsty, needing the bathroom, and feeling restless. There were many speakers but I was the first. The other speakers had been allotted 5–10 minutes each; I had 20 minutes for my story. I stepped onto the stage, took a deep breath, and began to speak. I had just started feeling comfortable when I realised that the clicker didn't work and I couldn't control the sequence of photos on the screen behind me. At first, I panicked because there were words on my slide that I hadn't memorised, and now I couldn't rely on the slides to help me. But after the first few slides, the tech guy signalled to me and started coordinating the slides with my talk for me. As I continued speaking, I felt more and more powerful and I could feel the support of the audience. That was a big realisation for me, the beginning of my new understanding that I actually love public speaking.

There were 11 or 12 other speakers but I was the only one who got a standing ovation. At that moment, I felt respected.

I also got hugs, many hugs, from the girls, and even from parents of other students.

My classmates came to me and looked at me as a hero. One of them, Nikita, one of my classmates from Russia, a very smart student and one of the other TED speakers, told me, "I never expected that it would be as hard as it was."

Another classmate, Mark, came up to me and said, "Jawid, you are still my best friend."

With the TED talk over and life back to normal, in class I was relieved to be able to be natural and relaxed with classmates. Instead of the heaviness of carrying my story in secret, a new lightness and humour was now possible. For example, there was one time when people were talking about their parents. One of my classmates said something about her dad, that her dad always told her not to worry about school stuff, that it would be fine and that she always had good grades. Another one responded, saying that her father always wants her to get good grades and so she is always worried about her grades. That was a moment when I felt the loneliness of being here without a family and I thought deeply about my dad, whom I have never seen. I became emotional for a moment but tried to find a way to release the emotion by talking about my dad. I joined in the conversation with a joke, "Thank God, I don't have a dad." They all laughed and thought it was funny. That was one way for me to release my emotions through laughter rather than tears.

It seems to me that even after the TED talk, I see myself as having two parts. One part, a social part, is smiling, making light of the fact that I don't have a dad to pressure me or praise me. But this is a mask that I have to wear to save my friends from seeing how upsetting it was for me to hear about their relationships with their dads. The mask hides how I feel. Underneath the mask, there is the real Jawid, sensitive, caring, observing, saving other people from discomfort by using humour.

Another example of how life at school changed after I told my story happened during a sports lesson. We were playing kickball and we had to run to the bases and touch the base before someone from the other team catches the ball and touches the base at the same time. As I was running, one of my teammates was cheering me on saying, "Run, Jawid, run for your life, run for your safety." When I heard that, I didn't feel insulted, angry, emotional, or sad.

That surprised me because before the TED talk, no one knew that part of my life, that there was a time when I was running for my life. This moment in the sports lesson was a change for me because both my classmates and I could be funny even about such a difficult topic, and I really enjoyed that.

A week after the TED talk, I was asked to do my speech again for the whole school as part of Refugee Awareness Week. This week had been planned by the Innovator Club before my TED talk. As a member of this club, I had spent many meetings with my friends discussing what activities should be included in that week. It was very awkward for me at those first meetings because they kept saying that they should find a refugee or someone who worked with refugees to come and talk to the school, without realising that there was a refugee sitting right there among them. At the same time, I was not ready to show them that I was a refugee and so I said instead, "I have many friends who are refugees and I could ask some of them to come." Also I said that I used to work as a volunteer in a refugee camp when I was in Athens and that a private school called Byron College had invited refugees who were living in camps to their campus for a day of activities, so I had a good idea of how to put together a good program for our week. It was really strange for me to say lies to my schoolmates since I had been among those refugees at the Byron College activity day.

We had spent four meetings without making any decisions about what our program should be. But after my talk, it became easier. Our teacher led us to the plan to have me give my speech again to the entire school. Before my speech, we would make a poster and write 'I welcome refugees because…' and just leave it so that everyone could finish the statement in any way they wanted. We also made some plans for reading books and telling stories to the students in the lower school.

I made some changes to my talk and once again I got a very warm reception from the audience. I was so comfortable this time; I was able to really engage the students who were my audience. I asked them questions and involved them in the story, especially my classmates who had become my biggest supporters in the community. The biggest change to my talk was that I spent more time describing Mr Welch and I gave him a very big thank you. It made me feel so good to acknowledge him in public for everything that he had done for me during the year.

The two times I told my story to the school made a huge change in my life. I could relax. I wasn't afraid of losing friends if anyone found out I was a refugee. In fact, students and their parents reached out to me to show their understanding and support. I began to feel like a real part of the community, that this was a place where I belonged. That also meant I could relax more deeply in my own life, since finally, I felt that I had a place. I started participating in many activities and felt like I could speak freely in my classes, especially when we had a unit on refugees in my humanities class and students turned to me so they could understand better.

I made some very good friends. One boy, Dani, had been my friend from my very first day at ISH; he reached out to me then and stayed very close throughout the year. He invited me to his house, introduced me to his parents, and was very eager to learn more details about my life and to try to understand the situation in Afghanistan. Another guy, Sedjro, was completely intrigued by my story. He wanted to know everything and he kept begging me to come and see the home where I lived; he also invited me to his house several times.

For the first time since I lived in Afghanistan, I felt like I was at home and surrounded by friends. I loved going to school and couldn't wait to get back to school on Monday mornings. Mr Welch remained my biggest supporter and I was very touched when he even mentioned me in his end-of-the-year talk to the school.

His daughter, Gaby, played a really influential role in my life. She was in the seventh grade, so several years younger than me. But she was so mature, not surprising, with a father like hers. She pulled me out of the hall one day to get me to join the Innovators' Club and that started our friendship. Actually, it is more true to say that she was like a little sister to me rather than just a friend. We never stopped laughing when we were together and we teased each other and played like little kids.

My close connection with Gaby continued into the summer. She invited me to her house one day and we did our usual things, playing and joking and teasing, running along the beach near her house. Then we returned home for dinner with her family. It was an amazing experience for me, being so comfortable with them, feeling such warmth from such a welcoming family. Mr Welch once again showed his big heart when he told me to just call him by his first name Peter since we were friends. This made a huge impression on me and I believe it is the beginning of a connection that will last a long time.

Chapter 12
Summer and Grade Nine

The summer passed quickly. I spent five weeks in Athens with my mother. During my first days there, I joined her in Nauplion along with several of her students, also refugees, who were participating in a scholarship program at the American College in Greece, as speakers at a conference on the education of refugees. Several days later, I joined some of her other students at another program sponsored by ACG for American university students who were in Athens to learn about the refugee situation in preparation for their careers in law enforcement and immigration. I went with her to her job and sat in the cafe there studying math in preparation for my next year's course. I was also reading several books to increase my fluency in English. I made friends with many of my mother's students and spent endless hours playing chess with my friend Dove. We also spent several days at beautiful beaches on the islands of Aegina and Angistri. I finally learned how to swim and learned how much fun it is to play in the sea on plastic mattresses.

It was also a very revealing summer for me, especially whenever I encountered refugees in the streets around Omonia and Viktoria. That had been me just a year earlier, and now here I was, like a tourist in Greece in the summer, getting ready to go back to a private school, studying math and English and chess, having conversations about what I might like to study when I go to university. The situation of many of the refugees I saw and spoke to struck me intensely, and I felt once again how lucky I was and at the same time felt so distressed that they didn't have the same opportunities and possibilities that I had. It was very hard for me to even remember that that had been my life because it's like that was a different Jawid and not the person I am now.

I really felt that when I volunteered several times at a shelter for unaccompanied minors, ages 8–12. I went with my friend Dove and we spent afternoons with them in different activities from football to watching movies. It was kind of a surreal experience for me to see kids in the same situation I had been in, and some in even worse, since they were much younger than I had been. And here I was, just one year out of such a shelter, and now volunteering for them and helping to give them a good time and some ways to adjust to their new lives. It also felt like a good way for me to pay back all the kindness people had shown to me when I was so vulnerable.

Then it was time for me to return to Finland to begin the new school year. I felt just like a normal kid, packing my new school clothes, getting back in touch with my school friends, being excited about my new courses. My mother and I headed to the airport for the flight back to Helsinki. Everything went smoothly, at least at the beginning. I checked in and headed to security. I made it through the initial check but then as I moved towards the scanning machines, two policemen approached me and asked to see my ID and my passport; they examined both documents closely. Clearly, the fact that my ID card showed that I was Afghan made me a target for them. But they signalled to me to continue and I finished my normal security check. Unfortunately, between that point and the final gate check, I was singled out five more times for very close scrutiny. I was devastated and angry. I felt that, finally, I was a normal person, going back to school just like thousands of other students but my past as a refugee kept catching up to me with each security check. It wasn't until I passed the final check at the gate that I could relax. I understand that the police were just doing their jobs and looking out for people who were being smuggled on false passports but even that didn't make up for the way it made me feel.

The first few weeks of school were some of the best of my life. I hadn't been back to the same school two years in a row since Afghanistan. I was so happy to see my friends and my teachers, to learn my schedule, and to sign up for fall sports. I attended all the beginning-of-the-year meetings; I didn't miss any of them, even when they were for new students and parents. I just wanted to be there all the time and take advantage of all the activities. And the time I spent on the outdoor overnight trip was unbelievable for me, since I had never even imagined that such things existed, and now here I was taking part, singing songs, going hiking, doing archery, swimming and jumping off the dock, canoeing, and lots of other games. The purpose of this was for all the students, old and new, to bond by having fun together. I enjoyed every minute of it and felt so proud when we played one game where we had to search for students with different talents and accomplishments. I was the one everyone ran to when we were called to "find students who are writing a book". My sense of belonging was powerful and helped me recover from my upset at the security checks at the airport.

This was a great year for me. No longer did I have to be careful to hide my true identity, I loved being open about who I was and what my story was, especially in humanities and English classes where we had an entire unit on the situation of refugees. I could tell that people thought I was an asset to the school and that was an indescribable feeling.

Far from feeling pulled in two directions, one a student at a private international school and the other a proud Afghan, I felt lucky. I loved both parts of my life and felt that they each made my life richer and deeper. A few weeks ago, my school was doing a service project while my class studied the issue of refugees in Finland. As part of that project, a visit to a refugee shelter was planned. Since it was a requirement, I went along. It actually ended up being a really fun and important afternoon for me. I entered the refugee centre with my classmates, laughing and looking forward to the visit. Once we got to the room where the plan was to play games with refugees, I started smiling; all the refugees were my friends.

For me it was a really significant moment when the two parts of my life were united.

I continued to do well in my studies; my English kept getting better and better. I figured out how to study, how to do presentations and projects, how to take tests and do labs. I couldn't be more grateful to ISH for providing me with this solid foundation for all my studies in the future.

My gratitude extends to the country of Finland and its people. I have a number of very good Finnish friends. Some help me with my math, the 91-year-old mother of another has knit hats and mittens for me, my guardian has shown numerous times that he understands me, the staff at my home keep me well fed and warm and safe. I am constantly amazed by this country that makes it look easy to get things done, and that has found ways to treat refugees with dignity. I am constantly impressed with the number of libraries in Finland and how they work to bring people together and offer such a wide range of services. The level of social services is so high that all citizens, including me, can feel that there is some security in their lives, and the level of respect for the laws and rules of life is very high. I love the saunas, the football fields, the swimming pools, the skating rinks, the beaches.

I am most of all grateful for the fact that this country has given me a residence permit and a passport. I am proud when I show people my Finnish alien passport and when people ask me where I live and I say I live in Finland without revealing my Afghan identity. It makes me feel like I am succeeding in the new direction of my life, the direction of figuring out my dreams and making them happen.

Chapter 13
Conclusion

There are several things that still surprise me.

One is how sometimes the smallest thing can send me back to my life in Afghanistan or to something that happened to me on my journey. One other aspect is my deep sense of what I have lost by leaving my family and my home. There is a big contrast with that, though, when I think of all the things that I have gained.

One day I was working in a lab during my science class. It required great precision in measuring the substances we were working with. I had an intense flashback, thinking of the time I worked at the sugar factory in my hometown. When I started working there, I was doing hard labour, using a sledgehammer to break the hardened dregs of the sugar from the previous year into tiny pieces and ultimately powder. But the manager knew me and remembered that I had been the top student in my class each year, so he changed my assignment and sent me to the lab where I assisted the workers there in measuring the sugar content of the solutions. I never imagined then that those skills would come in handy in a science class in a private school in Finland. The flashback moment was triggered when our class was doing an experiment and I instinctively tapped a test tube to release a gas bubble.

The biggest loss for me was my family. It becomes harder and harder to explain my life to them and it feels that that makes the distance between us even greater. I remember calling my brother Jawad on the way to my first trip to the dentist. "I'm getting my teeth cleaned," I told him. His response was to ask what that meant.

I am happy, I am safe, but I wonder when I will see them again. This past year my grandmother died. This hit me hard. I had been so close to her when she was living with us, and now I would never hear her voice again and was not able to mourn her together with my family. My sister has become engaged, and I know I will not be there for the wedding. I do hear a lot about the news from my village, my family, and my friends, and I am filled with sadness because much of that has to do with attacks and death, even of some of my closest friends from school. Whenever there is a new report of a bombing in Afghanistan, I shiver and am very anxious until I can get word that my family, my friends, and my home are safe.

Another big loss for me is the sense of being able to trust people. I have seen situations where human beings treated other human beings in the cruellest way possible. Sometimes it was a smuggler, other times a police officer or soldier, and other times a bureaucrat making decisions about people's lives in a cold way. This loss always feels to me like something that separates me from my friends, who don't have this deep feeling that to be safe they need to mistrust the motives of the person standing before them.

What I have gained, however, has been almost beyond my dreams. I now live in a country and continent at peace; I do not go to sleep thinking that a bomb may go off on the street outside my window. I am attending a school that is unlike anything I could have imagined when I was in Afghanistan, with its rigorous program that will prepare me well for university, with students from all around the world who will be my friends for life, with teachers and staff members and administrators who have gone far out of their way to take care of me and help me and ease me into a kind of education I had never known.

I can see a future for myself that could allow me to be almost anything I want. My experience has led me, as it has almost every other refugee, to want to work for human rights in one way or another. As a doctor? A lawyer? A businessman? A political leader? It is almost unbelievable that a little kid who ran barefoot through the streets of my village and sat on dirt to learn my lessons at school could end up at an Oxford or Harvard or Vanderbilt.

And yet, I know that I could, if I work hard enough and prepare myself in the right way. And after that, I could even end up going back to Afghanistan and working to bring peace and rebuild the country that I love so much. And my vision is even bigger; I would like to have an impact on the world, helping people suffering from natural disasters, dictators, from violations of their rights, who have lost all sense of dignity.

Today I am living in a society where there is equality between men and women. It is a relief for me to be able to hang out with the girls in my school just as easily as I can with the boys.

I have learned things about myself that I never knew. My love of public speaking. How sociable I am, that I can make friends easily with all ages and kinds of people. How resilient

I am, to have gone through the things I have gone through, and still be able to look at the world around me and the future ahead of me with curiosity and excitement. How I create a sense of family wherever I go; I am as comfortable on the streets of Athens with my friends as I am on the streets of Helsinki and I have people I trust and rely on in both cities. I have learned to hold in my emotions and control my responses to things that might agitate or upset me but I rely on the people I trust to calm me and help me work things through.

I have learned that it's best not to reveal my story until I know someone well. The easiest way to cut off a conversation with someone new is to say, "I'm a refugee"; their immediate reaction is to feel sorry for me or to be afraid of me. So, I rely on my status as a student at ISH or on my connection to my American mother as a cover story. And I wonder, how long does the label 'refugee' stick to a person? Will there come a time when that no longer will be the first thing people think when they learn my history?

And what of the three million refugees in Europe now? And the 71 million refugees in the world? Many of them are struggling with the basic needs of adequate food and housing. Others are isolated in camps that deprive them of the ability to find jobs or to learn about the new culture they have reached. Many of them are separated from their families, with mothers and fathers in Germany and children in Greece. Most ominously for the future, access to education is not assured for all. At the moment, only 3% of young refugees worldwide have access to higher education.

My story is their story, my need to be safe, to have dreams, to see paths to making my dreams come true. Each and every one of them has these same needs; the need to feel a sense of dignity again, a need to have a way to become self-sufficient and support a family, a desire to see their children have safe lives and an education that will allow them to make their mark on society. Are there policies in place that will make that happen? If not, why not? This is a western society that prizes diversity, writes constitutions and declarations that praise human rights and put into place institutions that make sure that all human beings can live with those rights. We refugees bring enormous talents and learning and experience to life here and just need help at this moment in time in finding our new balance here and gaining the opportunity to contribute in our own unique ways.

This was a book with a happy ending.

Chapter 14
January 2019

The day before it happened, I was at school. As a member of the student council, I was selling tickets for the Snow Ball. I was eager to be an example to other students by buying a ticket and getting them excited about the dance. At that moment, I had no idea that I would not be going to the dance after all. Everything was normal at school, being at school, complaining about teachers the way that kids do. The next day, after hanging out with my friends in the afternoon, I went home and had the longest conversation with my sister Sara in Afghanistan that I had ever had. She said, "Jawid, you know that your brothers don't want to leave Afghanistan even though the situation is getting really difficult." But she told me that she wanted to come because life was getting very hard, and it was almost impossible even to go out.

I was laughing at her saying, "You are engaged now. I cannot take responsibility for you; you will soon have a husband." This is how the conversation was going, laughing, joking, and making light of a difficult topic.

In the conversation she said, "Jawid, call your brothers. They always say you don't call them." I was laughing at what she said and I stubbornly told her that there were always problems with the internet when I called. What I didn't know then was that I would never again be able to talk to them.

The conversation with my sister lasted two hours.

That night I also talked to my mom and our whole conversation was about my brothers. I was saying how proud I am that they can survive in a place where the law of the jungle rules. That same night, I also called a girl who I wanted to take to the Snow Ball. She said yes! I felt really happy and when I went to bed, I tossed and turned with anticipation, thinking that finally my dream had come true. She would go to the Snow Ball with me in a beautiful dress and I would wear my suit.

The next morning around 5 am my phone rang. It was my brother Alijan. He was crying, sobbing, yelling, and telling me that we are destroyed, our lives have been ruined. I couldn't even ask him any questions. He was saying that he was trapped, his hands were tied and he didn't have a passport and so couldn't travel. He was saying that he was imprisoned in Finland, unable to leave. I could not understand what was going on and then he said, "Our brothers have been killed." He was saying that there is no one left in our family we could call our brothers. Afghanistan is not our home; all is lost.

I was completely shocked, numb, and paralysed. My throat collapsed, I couldn't speak, move, or react. I don't know how I moved from my room to get to the hallway. I cannot remember what happened but I realised at some point that four or five other boys had seen me and brought the staff members to see what was going on with me. I was on the floor and they were standing around me. I could hear my own voice but I couldn't feel anything. I was yelling, shouting, and hitting my head against the wall. Others came out of their rooms saying that they were trying to sleep. It was as though my senses did not function.

I kept saying to the staff members, "Get the tickets. Tickets, tickets." I couldn't say anything else, and then my phone started ringing. They answered it and spoke to Alijan. That is how they learned what had happened.

At that time, the only thing I could think of was to go back to Afghanistan. I cannot remember how long I was on the floor in the hallway, maybe two or three hours. For some time, I couldn't feel anything but after a while, I started checking Facebook. All my friends on Facebook were posting information about what had happened, even pictures of the bodies of my brothers were on Facebook; their bodies lying lifeless in the coffins, covered in a blanket, their faces bloody from the gunshots.

Those hours were the darkest time in my life. When my father was killed and my other brothers were killed and when my mother died, I was not old enough to feel the pain and the loss, but now, living alone in a foreign country, thousands of miles from home, the pain was unbearable. My brothers who sent me to safety, who gave their own freedom to save my life, were now gone. I couldn't reach out to my sister to comfort her, or to be there with their wives as they mourned the loss of their husbands.

I spent the next few hours in my room sitting on my bed, paralysed, not even able to cry. I couldn't believe that not even 12 hours earlier, I had been so happy, talking to my sister, my mom, making a date for Snow Ball. Now I wanted to punch the walls but I couldn't move. I spent that time staring at Facebook posts, looking at the pictures of my brothers' bodies, looking back at their messages to me, calling their numbers and sending them messages, hoping for a response that I knew I would never get.

In the meantime, Alijan had alerted the staff that Ali Soltani would come and pick me up and bring me to his home to be with his family. I really wanted to just be left alone but Ali Soltani would not leave me by myself. He understood how deeply I was wounded and he was worried about leaving me alone, worried that I might hurt myself. And he also understood that I needed to be around people who loved me, that I needed to be with an Afghan family so I could feel like I was in a real home again, like the one I had left behind. He was right, of course. It was better for me to be with them, eating Afghan food and speaking in Dari. But nothing could comfort me. I mostly stayed quiet, feeling awkward and speechless. I wanted to talk, to tell stories about my brothers and cry and laugh but I couldn't. Alijan had come down to Helsinki to join us but I couldn't talk to him either. We just kept looking at each other in disbelief and in grief. The only thing I remember talking about was that we wanted to go to Afghanistan immediately. We wanted to see our brothers' bodies, we wanted to go and fulfil our responsibilities as their brothers, but we couldn't. We both kept getting calls from our relatives in Afghanistan. When were we coming? We needed to be there to bury them as the only remaining male members of the family. Alijan didn't have a passport and neither one of us had enough money for a ticket.

Finally, late at night, Ali Soltani drove me home.

The next day Alijan went back up north to his home and his school. I got up late but managed to get my things ready and go to school. I cannot tell you how I got through that day or the day after that or the day after that. I sat in class, not understanding one thing. I hung out with my friends, silent, and unable to explain to them the reason I was like that. Some of them kept coming to me to ask why I was so sad, why I wasn't smiling. I didn't dare answer, I knew that if I said even the simplest thing, I would start crying and not be able to stop. The only thing I managed to do was when Taimi came up to me to ask me why I was so sad, and all I could say to her was that I just needed a hug.

Luckily, I already had a good connection with Ms Clarke and her office became a refuge for me. I spent a lot of time there, speaking to her and trying to make sense of what was going on. It was a comfort to me to know that I had a place at school where I could go when I needed to be alone or needed to talk. I also met on that Monday evening with Mr Welch. On Wednesday morning, my mother came from Athens.

Despite the care I was getting, I continued to suffer. I kept going to school and I spent a lot of time with my mother but all that was overshadowed by what I kept learning about what was going on in Afghanistan from the phone calls of my sister, my relatives, and my friends.

Alijan and I were overwhelmed with frustration; we felt the deep responsibility we had to our brothers, their home, their business, their wives and children, and to my sister. Our refugee status deprived us of the ability to go home and see our brothers buried, meet our responsibilities, and share our grief with our families. We also realised that neither one of us would survive long if we went back; we never learned the reason for my brothers' murders. We could easily become targets of it also, or targets of the Taliban, who consider any Afghan who has spent time in Europe as a traitor to be shot immediately. We felt hopeless, useless, and speechless as decisions were made there without our input. We felt guilt, living comfortable lives in Finland, getting a good education, looking at the promise of a good future, while there was nothing but despair for the family we had left behind.

The focus of all our feelings gradually centred on my brothers' wives and children. How would they manage without their husbands? The culture there is completely different from the culture here, and neither one of the two women had ever imagined life as anything other than the wife of Jawad or the wife of Ibrahim. There was no life insurance policy to help support them in the future. They had had limited education and they had never had the slightest preparation for a life where they would have to work to support themselves and their children. There was no one there to help. When my father died, Jawad had taken over as the head of the family to take care of my mother and the rest of us. He was 14 then. But his eldest child now was a daughter and only 11, so how could she help? And Ibrahim's child was just a baby. I had terrible visions when I tried to sleep at night. What would happen to these women? And what about the children? I imagined the worst. Would they become drug addicts? Suicide bombers? Shoe polishers in the market? Would the girls be raped or become pregnant while they were still children? Would the wives have to turn to prostitution to support their children? Would they end up begging in the streets? How would they all live without the love and support of a father and husband?

When I slept at night, in a comfortable bed, in a warm room, or when I drank hot tea or had a good meal, I kept thinking of the contrast between my life and what awaited them. What would happen to them now that they didn't have husbands to protect them? The situation did not remain static in Baghlan. There were reports that at least seven other people in the area were killed in a similar manner. And our house came under attack just a few days after my brothers were killed. It was really clear that the wives and children could not stay in their home anymore; they could easily become targets for rapists and murderers. But what could I do? How could I keep them safe? Alijan and I had endless conversations about this.

We kept coming back to the idea that we needed to go back to Afghanistan immediately.

Three things held us back, in addition to our political status and lack of money. Many adults in our lives kept repeatedly telling us that we could not go back, that it was too dangerous and that we would be killed. Hearing that over and over finally had an impact on us. The second argument was that we could do more for them from here to support them and keep them safe than if we went back. And the last argument was that finally relatives in Afghanistan had started making decisions that would keep the women and children safe, at least temporarily. Jawad's wife, Shukria, would go to her brother's house in Mazar Sharif with her five children, Ibrahim's wife, Zahra, would return to her father's house in our village with her baby, and my younger sister would go to live with my older sister in Mazar Sharif.

For us, this was a relief, a temporary but significant one.

It was very difficult, though. When news came that relatives had sold the kiosk that had been the major source of income for the families, it killed me, especially since I had been there at the very beginning of that business. I had started selling chewing gum to the villagers and from that, Jawad got the idea to add other products and finally had a store that supplied most villagers with everything they needed, fruits and vegetables, soap and cleaners, tools, ice cream and candy and cookies, bottles of gas. On top of that, my family home, the place where I was born and where I grew up, had to be returned to the guy we rented it from and a new family moved in just a few days after my brothers' deaths. In the space of just a day or two, the idea of home that I had treasured in my brain and heart throughout my journey and my time in Greece and Finland was wiped away. It felt like the ground had been opened up right under my feet. When I thought about the family being separated, with one sister-in-law in the north of Mazar and my sister in the south, and the other sister-in-law still in our village but back with her family, I could hardly breathe and found it hard to comprehend how my world could change so drastically in such a short time.

With all this going on, I almost forgot my grief and began to focus on coming up with a plan for what I could do to take on the responsibility of reuniting the wives and children and my sister in a safe place. I started talking with my school counsellor Ms Clarke, Alijan, my guardian, and with some refugee rights activists about ways that I could get them out of Afghanistan and bring them to Finland. The shocking thing to me was that no one told me it was impossible; most said that it would be very difficult and could take years. After a week of conversations, a plan began to take shape.

That plan was to ultimately ask Finland to allow them to join me and Alijan in Finland by getting a residence permit on the grounds that they would be re-joining their family here. The intermediate steps will be very difficult. Getting Afghan IDs and passports for the women and children is only the first hurdle and not an easy one at all. Once they obtain those, they will need to get to the Finnish embassy in New Delhi to put in their application for the residence permit, since the Finnish embassy in Kabul does not provide any client services. Getting them all to New Delhi will not be easy, how will they travel there? What will their status be there? Will we have to go there with them since they have no experience travelling, not even out of our village? Once we overcome those challenges, they will be able to file their Finnish residence application permit. That requires massive documentation. How do we manage that? And then once the application is filed, there will be a long waiting period before we get a response. If the answer is yes, they will come to Finland and then a whole new series of challenges arise. Where will they live? How will they adapt? How will we have to change our lives when they are here? And if the answer is no, then what?

I said that I almost forgot my grief while I was preoccupied with coming up with a plan, but the grief never really left, it just stayed there and caught up with me in the times when I let my guard down. And it stayed with me and had a huge impact on my life. I did continue to go to school every day but I couldn't concentrate on anything. Couldn't understand anything my teachers said in class, felt like I was in a different world from all my classmates, like I was a million miles away. I had no ability to do any work and I missed many classes when I slept too late, or when I was in the counsellor's office, or meeting with people at different NGOs or other agencies that help refugees, or when I was on the phone with the women in Afghanistan. Here I was, just weeks earlier I had been so happy when I learned that I made the honour roll, and now I couldn't do even the simplest assignment.

There were times when I tried to be my old self and hang out with my friends and laugh with them during recess and lunch. I did laugh and make jokes but it felt so fake like I was not being true to myself and even a little like I was disrespecting my brothers.

There were some things that helped me feel normal again. My teachers were really good about treating me as they always had. Just five days after I learned about my brothers, I attended parent-teacher conferences with my mother and it felt good to talk with my teachers about my work and what I had done well and how I could improve. It reminded me a little that life goes on.

One of the activities for my humanities and English classes was a play about refugees and how they were treated as they tried to integrate into Finnish society. This was the culmination of a months-long unit, and I was part of a group that wrote and acted in a play based on *Exit West*, one of the books we had read. I had been chosen as the main character, and the performance was on Wednesday, just a few days after my life changed so dramatically. I wasn't sure I'd be able to perform my part, would I be emotionally stable enough? Would some of the lines of the play trigger my grief and anger and make me forget everything and respond to those emotions rather than to the meaning of the play? Would I be able to remember my lines? Would I have the energy to be able to connect with the rest of the cast and with the audience? It turned out to be a very therapeutic experience for me. I held myself together and was able to use my sadness to deepen my performance and reach the audience with the important message of the play.

But there were just as many other things that made me lose it and plunged me back into my grief and anger and disbelief that my brothers were gone and into a feeling of being alone in the universe and that I didn't want to be there. A pain in my belly that was unbearable and made me want a knife to gouge it out. A howl that I hoped would remove the pain but when I opened my mouth, nothing came out. The only relief came when I smashed my phone to the tile floor, pounded on a mirror on the wall, pulled out my clothes and shredded them into pieces.

Three weeks later, things were calmer but my anger was increasing. The grief also remained, as deep and intense as ever. My classmates knew that something was wrong but had no idea of the actual reasons. They didn't know that, at the same time I was separating myself from them, I was scared I was losing them as my friends. They didn't know that I was afraid that I was going crazy. I knew that they were being hurt by the fact that I wasn't talking to them anymore. But I was also scared that they wouldn't be able to understand if they did know the whole story. And as much as I needed comfort from the people around me, I thought that they wouldn't be able to do that for me and that they would need comforting themselves when they heard the size of the tragedy that I was enduring. But despite all that, I finally decided that I had to explain to them what was going on with me because I didn't want to go on the way I had been, especially since rumours had started to spread. So, I made the decision, in the middle of another humanities and English class, in the midst of a discussion on leadership. The topic was the question of how leaders, like politicians, sometimes make statements and policies and then come to regret them and change them and what would we do, if we found ourselves in a similar situation? Would we make changes? We each had a few minutes to think about our answer and to write our response. I decided to use this as an opportunity to tell my classmates about what had happened in my family and to say that I regretted not telling them in the beginning. And so I stood up and told them. I was immediately relieved that I didn't have to hide the truth from them. I felt lighter and was really touched by their support and comfort.

Here I am, almost a month later, still in deep grief, beginning to be able to function normally again. I'm writing essays for school, studying for a math test, and finishing a report for PE. These activities, which just a month ago were the pieces of my normal school life, have become so difficult, it's hard to figure out why they matter. I've looked into darkness and am struggling to find my way back to the light and normality of a 16-year-old high-school student.

And I'm feeling intense frustration when I look at the situation from a bigger perspective. How can European laws say that my brothers' wives and children are not my family? How can Finland not see that this is an issue of women's rights and of protecting innocent children? Why is this so difficult? Why do Finland and the rest of Europe continue to deport Afghans back to a country that is overwhelmed by violence?

And I ache for my country. How much longer will there be war in Afghanistan? Is there any other country where two men, fathers and brothers, can be killed in front of their house and no police come, no investigation done? How much longer do we have to suffer like this?

My working draft of this book started with a very simple sentence, 'This is a story with a happy ending.' For months and months, anyone who read the draft started off with this idea. But now, after this past month, I deleted that sentence. Yes, in many ways, I am the luckiest of refugees, living in a country that treats me with dignity, going to a good school, and knowing I can continue my education however much I want. I have friends and people who love me deeply. I have all the material things I want and need. And I know that the quotation 'This is a story with a happy ending' might be true again in a few years. But right now, it's hard to even envision that. I'm not sure how I recover from my losses, how I move beyond my grief, and I'm not sure if I want to.

Epilogue

It is spring 2022. I am eager for the snow to finally melt in Helsinki. I am spending my days preparing for my IB (International Baccalaureate) exams and enjoying the company of my friends as we get ready to leave high school and scatter to universities all over the world.

I did recover from my grief and my huge sense of loss. My life on the surface now differs little from the lives of my friends. I have become completely comfortable with the comforts and customs of life in western Europe. I have worked through my grief and recovered from the trauma I suffered on my journey. I have made a life for myself here. I even have my family here now. We were successful in getting my sister-in-law Shukria and her 4 children to Finland, so I now have people near me who have known me since I was born, and young nieces and a nephew whom I adore.

But a new war has started and brought with it new waves of refugees. A reminder of all those old traumas of having to flee home for safety, arriving in new countries as a stranger in need of help, finding the energy and support to build a new life. An understanding that this kind of dislocation will keep repeating itself. A hope that somehow governments and peoples will discover and implement ways to treat these very vulnerable individuals and families with dignity and justice.

And then of course the events of last summer as the Taliban took over Afghanistan were difficult to comprehend. I understood then that my hope that there would be a time in the not distant future when I could go back and see my country again had been taken from me. I know now that it will be years and years, maybe even decades, before that could ever happen.

It is my hope that my book can join the stories and poems, films, videos, and paintings of other refugees in explaining the complexity of our lives and helping in some small way to increase the understanding of this experience and contribute to a greater acceptance of our common humanity.